# in
# my humble
# opinion.
# my
# so-called
# life

# soraya
# roberts

ecwpress

Published by ECW Press
665 Gerrard Street East
Toronto, Ontario, Canada M4M 1Y2
416-694-3348 / info@ecwpress.com

Editors for the press:
Jennifer Knoch and Crissy Calhoun
Cover and text design: David Gee
Series proofreader: Avril McMeekin

Library and Archives Canada
Cataloguing in Publication

Roberts, Soraya, author
In my humble opinion : My so-called life /
Soraya Roberts.

Issued in print and electronic formats.
ISBN 978-1-77041-308-5 (pbk.)
978-1-77090-881-9 (pdf)
978-1-77090-882-6 (epub)

1. My so-called life (Television program).
I. Title.

PN1992.77.M9R63 2016    791.45'72
C2016-902327-3    C2016-902328-1

Printing: Webcom    5  4  3  2  1
PRINTED AND BOUND IN CANADA

The publication of In My Humble Opinion has been generously supported by the Canada Council for the Arts which last year invested $153 million to bring the arts to Canadians throughout the country, and by the Government of Canada through the Canada Book Fund. Nous remercions le Conseil des arts du Canada de son soutien. L'an dernier, le Conseil a investi 153 millions de dollars pour mettre de l'art dans la vie des Canadiennes et des Canadiens de tout le pays. Ce livre est financé en partie par le gouvernement du Canada. We also acknowledge the Ontario Arts Council (OAC), an agency of the Government of Ontario, which last year funded 1,709 individual artists and 1,078 organizations in 204 communities across Ontario, for a total of $52.1 million, and the contribution of the Government of Ontario through the Ontario Book Publishing Tax Credit and the Ontario Media Development Corporation.

To my mom,
who hated this show,
but let it shape me anyway.

# Contents

# 1

## A Toaster or Something

Angela Chase was supposed to have a white lob — that's what *My So-Called Life* writer Winnie Holzman wanted: "albino white." "I may have seen a girl on the street, I really don't know," she says. "I guess it just occurred to me that 'Wow, that's out there.'" But the set hairdresser convinced her not to do it. She said it would ruin Claire Danes's hair, a natural dirty blond, and suggested arterial red instead. That meant every time Danes showered, she looked like "a murderess." And in a sense she was. Angela's red dye killed her past. A milk-colored mop might have been ideal as a symbol of her innocence — and, as a blank slate, a perfect metaphor for a girl searching for her identity — but it would have turned her into a specter floating seamlessly through her so-called life, the same way she always had. But red? Red is the color of revolution.

In her very first voice-over, Angela explains that, at 15, she is done with her old life. "Things were getting to me," she says, peering out from two peanut-colored curtains of hair. "Just how people are, how they always expect you to be a certain way." A subsequent scene in the pilot has her staring wide-eyed at her own reflection as a newly dyed blood-colored hank drips over her shoulder. "School is a battlefield, for your heart," she says. "So when Rayanne Graff told me my hair was holding me back, I had to listen. 'Cause she wasn't just talking about my hair. She was talking about my life." By changing her hair, by taking control of it, she is taking control of that life, the life her parents and her teachers and the world have been dictating for her. The red signals her search for her own persona — a bright new one beyond her inheritance — even though she's not entirely sure what it is yet. As she tries to find out, Crimson Glow illuminates her way.

Angela Chase appeared on ABC for the first time on August 25, 1994. She was nothing like her contemporaries, most notably hair-flipping cheerleader Kelly Kapowski and designer uber-bitch Brenda Walsh. Both *Saved by the Bell* (1989–1993) and *Beverly Hills, 90210* (1990–2000) were glossy, brightly colored celebrations of Hollywoodized teen life. These "adolescents" always looked amazing and were amazingly popular and lived in amazing houses with amazing parents and went to amazing parties and dated amazing guys and it was all so exciting! And when the music turned sober, these beautiful young things preached from their gilded screens about safe sex and just saying no. Even the ostensibly real teens in Canada's *Degrassi* franchise were contrived. With no sheen whatsoever (the show even excluded contemporary cultural references in an attempt to avoid becoming dated — it didn't work), the original CBC trilogy used a documentary-like aesthetic to shoot a Toronto school's frayed halls, filled with average-looking kids with average homes. But the show's unwavering devotion to social issues, ranging from alcoholism to suicide to homophobia to anorexia, made it seem more like a series of thinly disguised public service announcements than entertainment.

If anything, Angela is the double-x answer to *The Wonder Years'* Kevin Arnold, narrating her own search for personhood. The idea for *MSCL* actually predated the Fred Savage nostal-giungsroman. Marshall Herskovitz and Ed Zwick conceived *MSCL* back in the '70s while they were working on ABC's *Family*, a drama co-starring Kristy McNichol as a girl named Buddy. "Marshall and Ed would think of ideas for this teenage girl character," Holzman says, "like she lied to her parents or she experiments with cigarette smoking, or whatever it was — and the showrunner would come back to them and say, 'That's not our Buddy.'" So they decided, "Let's do a teenage girl but make her super authentic like everything we couldn't do on *Family*." Though they were sidelined by their next show, *thirtysomething*, once it ended in 1991, they brought the idea to Holzman, one of its writers. She's the one who conjured Angela Chase, the Pittsburgh adolescent with the very un-amazing life, and surrounded her with an equally relatable entourage — best friends Rayanne Graff and Rickie Vasquez, crush Jordan

Catalano, ex-BFF Sharon Cherski, neighbor Brian Krakow. Sure, social issues came up, but, as in real life, they weaved through the narrative, never didactically, but as mere fragments of a multi-faceted existence that often went unresolved. "I wanted [Angela] to be given her due as a human being and as someone to be respected and allowed her own complexities," Holzman says. "I felt that way about every character."

Human beings are hard to find on TV — ambiguity was rare on primetime in the '90s and continues to be even now. But on *MSCL*, not having the answer was allowed, nay encouraged. In the pilot, Angela is asked why she is quitting yearbook and she says, with irritation, "I don't know why." To allow for uncertainty is a hallmark of maturity. The inability to easily categorize ourselves is what makes us human, and, according to Holzman, it is one of the main components of *MSCL*. ("Why're you like this?" Jordan asks Angela in "Life of Brian." "Like what?" she responds. "Like how you are?") It is also a main component of feminism, which, in Tavi Gevinson's words, "is not a rulebook but a discussion, a conversation, a process." In fact, the founder of the teen feminist mag *Rookie* delivered a TEDx Talk in 2012 called "Still Figuring It Out," in which she discussed *Rookie*'s encouragement of equivocation. "The point is not to give girls the answers and not even give them permission to find the answers themselves," she said, "but hopefully inspire them to understand that they can give themselves that permission, they can ask their own questions, find their own answer." Because one answer does not exist. "Women are complicated, women are multi-faceted," Gevinson said. "Not because women are crazy but because people are crazy and women happen to be people." She noted that "teenagers are especially contradictory"[1] but she only really saw that reflected on television in *Freaks and Geeks'* Lindsay Weir and *MSCL's* Angela Chase. The latter is particularly ambivalent, often contemplating one thing and doing another. "What I was thinking, as, like, a New Year's resolution, is to stop getting so caught up in my own thoughts, 'cause I'm, like, way too introspective, I think," she says in "Resolutions." "But what if not thinking turns me into this really shallow person? I better rethink this becoming less introspective thing."

Angela's thoughts, her life, filled a hole in the market. Holzman knew the Hollywood stereotypes around her and created a show within them. "I would try to almost have them and then bust people out of them," she says. She took the one-dimensional, gave it complexity, and in so doing produced one of the first feminist teen series. *MSCL* never once uses the F-word, but at the moment third-wave feminists in the real world were questioning the traditions surrounding gender, sexuality, class, and race, *MSCL* was doing the same thing on TV. In a neat parallel with the movement, the show's teen protagonists personify powerlessness in the face of authority. While Angela and her friends attempt to establish independence, they constantly knock against the rules established generations before them.

---

1 As Nomy Lamm wrote in "It's a Big Fat Revolution" in the formative third-wave collection, *Listen Up: Voices from the Next Feminist Generation* (1995): "My contradictions can coexist, cuz they exist inside of me, and I'm not gonna simplify them so that they fit into the linear, analytical pattern that I know they're supposed to."

There is, however, one historical figure Angela's creators pledged whole-hearted allegiance to: Holden Caulfield. Describing the show's title as "Salingeresque," Matt Zoller Seitz wrote in an oft-quoted review in the *New York Times* that *My So-Called Life* "showcases the most sophisticated use of the unreliable narrator ever seen in network drama." Like Holden's narration in *Catcher in the Rye*, Angela's, he wrote, "shows how teenagers try to control their chaotic inner lives by naming things, defining them, generalizing about them, even when they don't really understand what they're going through." The results tend to be unintentionally funny. "We barely talked, so when we did, it came out sounding really meaningful," Angela narrates in "Self-Esteem" before announcing out loud: "There's a tiny leaf in your hair." In "Life of Brian," she claims to respect Jordan Catalano for operating under the mantra of "whatever happens, happens," but when Brian Krakow uses the same expression, she claims it's "the stupidest thing" she's ever heard. These are the sorts of inconsistencies that are not uncommon in everyday life, but their complexity often inspires Hollywood neglect. The narrator is traditionally considered the authority, the one with objectivity — their word is the last word, and it's never wrong. *MSCL* operates under no such pretenses. Its creators force us to live through Angela's contradictions with her — when she is wrong, when she is right, when she is both and neither — because it is through her voice-over, through her particular perspective, that we experience everything on-screen. "Diaries are records of emotional rather than factual memory, and Angela's narration is unreliable because she's recording subjective experiences rather than objective truths,"[2] writes Caryn Murphy in "It Only Got Teenage Girls" in the critical essay collection *Dear Angela: Remembering My So-Called Life*. "The viewer is often privy to information that Angela either doesn't know or doesn't want to see, which helps to establish her as a 'realistic' adolescent."

The real Claire Danes was all of 13 years old when she auditioned for *MSCL*. Winnie Holzman had written a pilot that was meant to capture "a naked quality, not a person but a feeling of freedom and bondage, shyness and fearlessness," which the young actress perfectly embodied. At her audition in 1992, Danes, Holzman recalled years later in the *New Yorker*, "was sexy and not sexy, free and bound up, open and closed, funny and frighteningly serious." Writer John Lahr, who spoke to Holzman for the magazine in 2013, defined Danes's acting as "a combination of thoughtfulness and impulsiveness" and what better way to describe Angela Chase? "I don't think I've ever played a character who was having such a parallel experience," Danes said in an interview for the DVD collection *My So-Called Life: The Complete Series*. She filmed the pilot in early 1993 and ABC first mentioned *MSCL* to the *Times* in April, calling it the "anti-*90210*." There was talk of a midseason pickup, but, Herskovitz said, "they don't really have a place for it." The network took almost a year to find one, and in May 1994 it was announced that *MSCL* would appear that fall on Thursdays at 8 p.m. By that time, Danes was 15 like her character. "Angela and

---

2 This recalls a line from Jennifer DiMarco's essay "Word Warrior" from *Listen Up*, in which she describes her diary as "a place where the truth could be my own."

I were the same age, so we could dance around each other," she told the *New Yorker*. "Sometimes I would have an experience and then it would be articulated in the show. Other times, I would play it out, then experience it personally later." Both she and her character took themselves seriously, but they also felt repressed by the line they toed. "I remember being so relieved that I had an opportunity to voice my complaints about my time at school so perfectly and so eloquently," Danes said, "with the right amount of rage and humor."

But she couldn't have done it without Holzman, and Holzman couldn't have done it without her. "We gave birth to each other," the writer told Lahr. "I was looking at someone who literally could do anything, and so I could too." Timing did, however, play a pivotal role. If Holzman had auditioned an older Danes, their meeting might not have been so serendipitous. It was that fleeting elixir of adolescent energy that synergistically bonded Claire Danes and Angela Chase. The result? The pinnacle of Danes's acting career, the sole instance in which she and her character would be so fluidly continuous, imbuing her with a rare power (at any age, let alone 13): the ability to shape the show around her. Because Danes was underage, she could only spend a small amount of time on set, which translated to a limited amount of time viewers could spend with Angela. If she were hired, it would mean changing the focus of the show to include her family (uptight mother Patty, indecisive dad Graham, bratty sister Danielle) and friends. And so it changed: Danes, at 13, dictated the production of an entire TV series — she was that good.

Bringing her in meant chucking out the show's initial diary concept. When Holzman was originally hired by Herskovitz and Zwick, *MSCL* was supposed to unfurl around a teenager's journal. Holzman consequently began by writing a diary in a voice that captured the "sense memories" she had formed as a teenager (a theater geek in high school, she used the Stanislavski method). Though the idea was eventually dropped, some of her entries bubbled back up in the form of Angela's voice-overs. And the show's epistolary foundation is enforced by numerous allusions to Anne Frank's *The Diary of a Young Girl*, including the juxtaposition of Angela's face with that of the young Dutch writer who recorded her experience hiding from the Nazis as a 13- to 15-year-old (eerily, the same age span as actress Claire Danes when she played Angela Chase). "She says, 'I,'" a teacher reminds Angela's class of Anne Frank (and us of Angela) in the pilot. Thus Angela thinks of Frank as "lucky," because her agency, her "I," is what Angela aspires to — even when Angela's in the room, her parents often speak of her in the third person. At the end of *MSCL*'s first episode, Angela even characterizes Frank, who eventually died in the camps, as liberated: "She was hiding. But in this other way she wasn't. She'd, like, stopped hiding. She was free." Frank had committed the ultimate political act — transcending confinement by freeing herself within the pages of her diary. Though feminist critic Katha Pollitt argued that "'the personal is political' did not mean that personal testimony, impressions, and feelings are all you need to make a political argument," in *Manifesta: Young Women, Feminism, and the Future*, the seminal introduction to third-wave feminism,

Jennifer Baumgardner and Amy Richards qualified this: "It may not be all you need, but testimony is where feminism starts." And it is where *MSCL* starts too. "I am a feminist, they are feminists," Holzman says of Herskovitz and Zwick, "so there's no doubt that there's a feminism at work in the idea for the show and in the DNA of the show."

The year before *MSCL* started shooting, a 22-year-old university student named Rebecca Walker coined the term "third wave" in *Ms.* magazine. Her call-to-arms was spurred on by attorney Anita Hill, who had accused Clarence Thomas, her supervisor at the U.S. Department of Education and the Equal Employment Opportunity Commission, of sexual harassment. "Can a woman's voice, a woman's sense of self-worth and injustice, challenge a structure predicated upon the subjugation of our gender?" Walker inquired. "Anita Hill's testimony threatened to do that and more." But ultimately it didn't. Ultimately, Hill's credibility was questioned — the length of time it took her to come forward, her continued contact with Thomas — and the man she attempted to fell enjoyed a cushiony landing on the Supreme Court. Her testimony wasn't enough. "Thomas's confirmation, the ultimate rally of support for the male paradigm of harassment, sends a clear message to women: 'Shut up! Even if you speak, we will not listen,'" Walker wrote. "I will not be silenced."

Though feminism is traditionally defined as equality for both sexes in social, political, and economic spheres,[3] Walker

---

3 Feminists tend to prefer bell hooks's definition: "Feminism is a movement to end sexism, sexist exploitation, and oppression."

adapted it to her generation. This was no longer the first-wave suffragettes (they went out in the '20s) or the second-wave women's libbers (they lasted into the '80s), this was what the *Times* had prematurely deemed the "postfeminist era." "To be a feminist is to integrate an ideology of equality and female empowerment into the very fiber of my life," Walker wrote in response to the *Times*. And this didn't just apply to women anymore, it applied to girls too. According to *Manifesta*, psychologist Carol Gilligan helped usher in the girls' movement by stressing the importance of surfacing young women's interior monologues. In the prologue to her 1990 book *Making Connections*, Gilligan wrote that she was "changing a tradition by including girls' voices." And the riot grrrls picked up where she left off. The young punk feminists from the Northwestern U.S. reclaimed epithets like "slut" and "bitch" and empowered teens with music and art and zines. Bratmobile coined "riot grrrl" in one of these zines, and in another written by Bikini Kill's Kathleen Hanna in 1991, the riot grrrl manifesto exposed "racism, able-bodieism, ageism, speciesism, classism, thinism, sexism, anti-Semitism, and heterosexism." Meanwhile, Baumgardner and Richards and their Third Wave *Manifesta* called "to liberate adolescents from slut-bashing, listless educators, sexual harassment, and bullying at school, as well as violence in all walks of life, and the silence that hangs over adolescents' heads, often keeping them isolated, lonely, and indifferent to the world."

*MSCL* broke this silence on a much larger scale than activists and academia. As a primetime TV show, it was accessible to a wider audience, like the riot grrrls' music, but, unlike the riot grrrls, it delivered the message through actual teenagers. If the third wave encouraged girls to speak up, Angela Chase was their spokeswoman. Even her name itself, Angela, is derived from the Greek word for "messenger of God." She is the chosen one. Her voice echoes through Pennsylvania's Liberty High School, through her own home, through that of her best friend Rayanne Graff, through Rickie Vasquez's head, through Jordan Catalano's heart, through Brian Krakow's everything. Whether it is her actual voice or the one inside her or the one written down, we hear it all, it all has value. The show even used a separate tack for filming Claire Danes in voice-over, a wide lens focused on her face to give the impression of intimacy. It was "a psychic space around her so we're inside her experience," according to one of the producers. But even outside her head, in the final scene of the pilot, the camera and the cast whirl around Angela. She is the center of this universe.

In *MSCL*'s very first scene, Angela looks directly at the viewer and says, "Um, excuse me." Her first words are an apology despite having done nothing wrong. This is the old Angela, the one who accepts the world she has been dealt, the girl at the beginning of "The Fable":

> *Once upon a time there lived a girl. She slept in a lovely little cottage made of gingerbread and candy. She was always asleep. One morning she woke up, and the candy had mold on it. Her father blew her a kiss and the house fell down. She realized she was lost. She found herself walking*

*down a crowded street. But the people were made of paper.*
*Like paper dolls. She blew everyone a kiss goodbye and*
*watched as they blew away.*

This is Angela Chase's portrait of her awakening, which appears in "The Substitute" in her school magazine, the *Liberty Lit*. The gingerbread-and-candy cottage houses the "good" girl, a sweet girl who works on yearbook, whose best friend is the daughter of her mom's best friend, whose warm (in color, even) suburban two-parent family is equally pleasant. It's a life without edge, one with simple rules — about friends, about family, about the world — that are followed without question. It's a wholesome existence in which the chaste Chases fit perfectly. Except there's something off about it. At the brink of adulthood, Angela suddenly realizes that her life is so precariously unidimensional that one kiss could dismantle the whole thing. "It just seems like you agree to have a certain personality or something, for no reason, just to make things easier for everyone," she says in the pilot. "But when you think about it, I mean, how do you know it's even you?"

Who Angela is is indistinguishable from how she sounds. Her voice is her source of power. It's all she really has, and it's what gives shape to her existence, and thus the show itself. Angela's voice is so distinct that when she and Rayanne break up, Rayanne can no longer bear to hear her friend's old expressions. "Don't say, 'In my humble opinion,'" she tells Rickie in "In Dreams Begin Responsibilities." "That's Angela talk. That's how Angela Chase talks. What are you trying to do, depress me?" Angela's voice is an emotional barometer. When she is around Jordan Catalano, she cannot control it. "If only there was a button somewhere that I could just push to force me to stop talking," she says. And when she's angry, she clams up, weaponizing her silence the way only a teenager is allowed. When her best friend betrays her and then calls out to her, she doesn't answer ("When you call someone's name, like, kind of loud and they don't hear you? It makes you feel really lonely," Angela says prophetically in "Betrayal"). When Jordan babbles an incoherent apology, she simply stares. But it's her choice. Like Rebecca Walker, she will not be silenced by anyone but herself. So when her principal attempts to shut her, and her classmates, up in "The Substitute" by shutting down the *Liberty Lit*, she does anything but. And when she fights with Jordan in the last episode, it's through her words. In a recurring dream, Angela confronts him after he betrays her, screaming with so much power that her face contorts into a grimace. She doesn't hit him; she doesn't need to, her voice packs enough of a punch.[4] "Then I wake up," she says. "The storm of words still pounds through my body."

It's a line worthy of Vic Racine, *MSCL*'s response to *Dead Poets Society*, whose sign-off is "question everything."[5] The substitute specifically steers Angela and her friends away from "false, fake, boring, synthetic, bogus" non-expression toward

---

4 Ellen Neuborne writes in the *Listen Up* essay "Imagine My Surprise," "listen for the jerk who will tell you to lower your voice. Tell him to get used to the noise. The next generation is coming."

5 bell hooks would love Vic. Her 1994 book *Teaching to Transgress: Education as the Practice of Freedom* promoted collaborative learning over authoritarian rule.

a more emotive form. "I want anger. I want honesty. I want nakedness," he says in the aptly named "The Substitute." "What you feel like saying, write it down instead." He's the perfect teacher for a diarist manqué; no wonder Angela tells her parents, "He's an adult I can look up to, finally." While her mom and dad fought for civil rights in the '60s and ostensibly want her to stand up for her own, their values have become more conservative with age (a recurring theme among characters in the on-screen universes of Zwick and Herskovitz). Now they are more concerned with their daughter getting suspended than freeing her mind. Vic is not. Vic talks the talk and walks the walk to the point that he encourages Angela to actually walk out on school. He wears one white sock and one black, he chews toothpicks, and he inspires his entire class to follow suit, turning them into his own personal quasi-cult. He even throws out their old work (literally, out the window), which is met with criticism from Angela, who has not quite shrugged off her parents' beliefs early in the episode. "I did it to clear the slate. I did it to wake you up," Vic explains. "I did it to do something, to find you. And now, guess what, here you are, wide awake in front of me."

Angela's awakening equates to finding her own voice, which leads to her supporting others to find theirs, her version of political engagement. Thus, Angela's self-expression is a form of activism, like *MSCL* itself. It is particularly symbolic that Angela risks suspension for the first time to fight censorship by publishing the *Liberty Lit* and with it the "naked" voices of the students that the principal deems "unacceptable." "I mean, what is the point of school if you can't say what you're thinking," she tells her parents. "You told me to pick my battles. Well, this is it. It may not be a war protest or a civil rights demonstration, but it's all I've got." But if this — giving the voiceless a voice, the invisible visibility — is not a political act, then what is? Like its feminist predecessors, *MSCL* makes the personal political, turning a teen girl's internal life and the nuances of her existence (and that of her family and friends) into something worth fighting for. School may be a battlefield for your heart, but it is a battlefield for your identity too. And the ultimate triumph — after 19 episodes of war — is nothing more than who you are. "People always say you should be yourself, like yourself is this definite thing, like a toaster, or something. Like you can know what it is," Angela says in voice-over in "Pressure." "But every so often, I'll have, like, a moment, where being myself, and my life right where I am is, like, enough."

And it was more than enough for everyone else. She was only 15 years old, but Angela Chase didn't just start her own revolution. Without her, there would be no Buffy Summers, no Veronica Mars, no Felicity Porter — and her influence continues to this day. As Claire Danes herself said almost 20 years later as CIA agent Carrie Mathison in *Homeland*, "Sit the fuck down! I'm not finished."

# 2

## It Hurts to Look at You

Angela Chase is leaning. She wears an outfit borrowed from her new best friend — bustier, miniskirt, studded belt — covered by one of her own plaid shirts, a newly minted uniform to go with her newly dyed hair. She is thinking, having been asked for her ideal pre-coital conversation (something, "like, romantic"). Head cocked, looking off into the distance, she says dreamily, as if the words were emanating from her very soul, "You're so beautiful, it hurts to look at you."

From the start, *My So-Called Life*'s relationship with beauty was fraught. Former child model Alicia Silverstone initially auditioned for the role of Angela Chase, and creator Ed Zwick wanted her, but creator Marshall Herskovitz did not. "Alicia is so beautiful that that would have affected her experience of the world," he told the *New Yorker* in 2013. "You can't put that face on what's been written for this girl." Claire Danes was more malleable. She met the script's very precise requirement of transforming "in an instant from beautiful to ordinary." Danes was to '90s teen TV what Molly Ringwald was to '80s teen movies. A decade before *MSCL* premiered, John Hughes claimed he had been inspired by Ringwald's headshot, which showed a pouty freckle-faced redhead, to write *Sixteen Candles*. He banked on her "charismatic normality," as film critic Pauline Kael put it, in half the films that made up his teen canon. Similarly, in the midst of '90s television's Swatch dogs and Diet Coke heads — the impeccably made-up Beverly Hills denizens of *90210*, the brunette beauties of *Party of Five*, the porcelain blonds of *Sweet Valley High* — Angela and her friends offered up a new kind of clique. None of *MSCL*'s central female characters are presented as ideals of beauty, because ideals of beauty don't exist here. "Sometimes it seems like we're all living in some kind of prison. And the crime is how much we hate ourselves," says Angela in "The Zit," putting a poetic spin on perhaps the most universal theme of young adulthood — the feeling that we don't belong — and the show's attempt to correct it. "It's good to get really dressed up once in a while and admit the truth: that when you really look closely? People are so strange and so complicated that they're actually beautiful."

You don't have to look too closely at Jordan Catalano to know that. Ideals of beauty may not exist, but he comes pretty close. His embodiment of physical perfection remains out of reach for almost everyone in the series — even the men. ("I think you'd better prepare yourself," Patty tells her husband in "Why Jordan Can't Read." "I get the definite feeling this kid is very good looking.") Angela is the exception. She is the one who convention has designated Jordan's physical opposite, yet she's the only one who can get near him. It's a twist worthy of Shakespeare:

> *My mistress' eyes are nothing like the sun;*
> *Coral is far more red than her lips' red;*
> *If snow be white, why then her breasts are dun;*
> *If hairs be wires, black wires grow on her head.*
> *I have seen roses damask'd, red and white,*
> *But no such roses see I in her cheeks;*
> *And in some perfumes is there more delight*
> *Than in the breath that from my mistress reeks.*
> *I love to hear her speak, yet well I know*
> *That music hath a far more pleasing sound;*
> *I grant I never saw a goddess go;*
> *My mistress, when she walks, treads on the ground:*
> > *And yet, by heaven, I think my love as rare*
> > *As any she belied with false compare.*

Jordan encounters "Sonnet 130" in English class and recognizes Angela in it. Where he is the physical ideal, she is the ideal non-ideal. Shakespeare's mistress is not "physically perfect," but that is precisely why she is so precious; as Brian Krakow explains (when Jordan cannot), "She's not just a fantasy. She's got, like, flaws. She's real."

But the specter of the flawless fantasy hangs over Angela as it does over us all. In *Manifesta*, Jennifer Baumgardner and Amy Richards call this the feminist dilemma: "One's looks, or lack thereof, affect how one experiences life as a woman." One of the defining texts of the third wave, Naomi Wolf's 1990 pulchritreatise *The Beauty Myth*, argues that the more "hindrances women have broken through, the more strictly and heavily and cruelly images of female beauty have come to weigh upon us." As proof, she points to the rise over the years in pornography, cosmetic surgery, and eating disorders (in *MSCL*'s nod to this thinsposphere, a trio of teen girls talk in the foreground of one scene about the difference between "fat-free" and "nonfat"). "More women have more money and power and scope and legal recognition than we have ever had before," Wolf writes, "but in terms of how we feel about ourselves physically, we may actually be worse off than our unliberated grandmothers." Or our liberated mothers.

Angela's mom is a former prom queen who, in Rayanne's mom's words, looks like "a commercial for something really clean." Meanwhile her daughter doesn't even make enough of an impression to appear on the "Sophomore Girls: The Top 40" list — collated by Liberty High's jocks — which makes her perfect 10 of a mom sad. It makes Angela sad too. She categorizes herself as "ugly" because she is not, like her mother, a blond with a pert nose. "You expect me to be beautiful, because you're beautiful," she tells Patty in "The Zit." Naomi Wolf doesn't blame Patty, she blames the "iron maiden," the standard women are encouraged to attain despite its unattainability. "The worst feeling is suddenly realizing you don't measure up," says Angela, "and in the past when you thought you did, you were a fool." The top 40 list's most beautiful, for instance, is a thin blond with pleasant features and a string of pearls. "Casey Hall is the prettiest girl in our class," Angela says. "Maybe even the whole school. Maybe even in America." Her statement isn't so hyperbolic when you consider the national ideal. In the same episode, a magazine called *American Gal* features yet another thin blond. "This girl is everywhere," Patty says. "Perfect face. Perfect body." In one scene, the model actually comes alive, and Angela is struck dumb as the cover girl laments her perfect life. "I don't have to go to the bathroom, ever," she trills. Her comment recalls Alisa L. Valdes's *Listen Up* essay "Ruminations of a Feminist Aerobics Instructor": "If a woman of Barbie's proportions existed, she wouldn't be able to walk, breathe, or digest food."

Barbie's cloud of electric pink sparkle dust obscures reality to the point that a blemish can eclipse the sun. "It was all I could feel, all I could think about," Angela says of her solitary pimple. "It blotted out the rest of my face, the rest of my life. Like the zit had become the truth about me." After expending all her energy on her face, Angela has nothing left for anything else. As Abra Fortune Chernik wrote in *Listen Up*'s "The Body Politic" of her own eating disorder, she was "the physical ideal because she was starving, self-obsessed, and powerless, a woman called beautiful because she threatened no one except herself." When we *are* a threat, it's to other women. Angela shames Sharon for being on the top 40 list for best hooters, but only because she is jealous. Ironically, Sharon envies Angela for being flat. As always, the ideal is anything we are not.

Had Claire Danes been born with a different body, Angela Chase would have been an entirely different person — Danes's body is as intrinsic to forming her character as is her voice. As John Lahr wrote in his *New Yorker* profile of Danes in 2013, "In extremis or out of it, her body semaphores feeling." Angela is always poised, yet always moving. When she is happy, she is happy with her whole being. In one particularly memorable scene in "Why Jordan Can't Read," after the second time Angela and Jordan kiss in his car, Danes performs a little "impromptu ballet" in the Chases' front yard. At the time, she did it without music, buoyed by the headiness of the moment. "I had to find something that caught her emotion and played musically with her as she spun around and went through this absolute emotional elation," *MSCL* composer W.G. Snuffy Walden said in *The Complete Series*. The scene takes place at night in the empty front yard of a glowing house, and, with the camera watching from afar, Angela looks like a figure in a life-sized music box. And that's the sound Walden chose, a simple glockenspiel-like melody, reminiscent of the tune to which a tiny ballerina twirls without a care in the world.

Sad Angela is just as affecting. She curls up on the floor or lies prostrate on her bed, her arms stretched out as if in sacrifice on some hormonal altar. "A testament to Danes's knack for self-exposure is her willingness to look ugly," Sasha Weiss wrote in the *New Yorker* in 2012. "This mood-swinging is the essence of her acting, and so it's also the thing that people like to make fun of." Hence the Claire Danes Cry Face Project, a Tumblr tribute devoted to every scene in which her face collapses into a chin-trembling sob. While Danes has called the process of physicalizing her roles "mysterious," she started training as a dancer at only six years old. "Dancing is a kind of drawing. I'm interpreting what I'm hearing with my body," she told the *New Yorker*. "Acting is like that too." It's also a rejection of the small physical space women are traditionally expected to occupy.

In *Throwing Like a Girl* (1990), third-wave feminist Iris Marion Young explored the ways in which women physically hold themselves differently from men. She parsed the female body's socialized burden, acquired at puberty — Angela's breasts coming between her and her father, for instance — a subject that Simone de Beauvoir introduced in *The Second Sex* (1949). Women often "fail to summon the full possibilities of our muscular coordination, position, poise, and bearing," Young wrote. They take shorter steps. They keep their arms close, their legs too. But Angela is different. Angela's gait is as changeable as her expressions. According to Winnie Holzman on *The Complete Series*, Danes had a habit of straying from her mark while shooting *MSCL*, a testament to her ability to break free from her socialized burden. Brian is similarly dynamic, flitting between ramrod alertness and hunchbacked lovesickness. Rayanne's bearing, meanwhile, is as masculine as her approach to the opposite sex — she almost manspreads (20 years before the *Oxford Dictionary* recognized the word) — while Sharon has a staccato gait in step with her bubbly persona, and Rickie is skittishly elegant. Then there's Jordan, who, along with his languid lean, exudes a certain grace, an airy musicality.

Like her movement, Angela's garb contains multitudes (both literally and otherwise). Despite her crush on Liberty High's resident James Dean, Angela is forever fighting for the possibility that we are more than we appear, and her weapon is her wardrobe. While clothing defines us to a certain extent throughout our lives, it is particularly descriptive in adolescence when we are choosing our identities. At Angela's age, selecting a shirt is tantamount to selecting who she is. To reflect her persona, *MSCL* costume designer Patrick Norris layered her outfits — unoriginal items mixed with the unexpected — without overdoing it. "She was so deep internally that I never wanted her clothes to really outshine who she was, you know?" he told *Vulture*. Her distinctly unisex style can be traced back to two gender-bending icons. "I was thinking about the grunge movement and Kurt Cobain, but also the softness and silhouettes in *Annie Hall*. I thought if I could blend something like that together, I could give her this whole kind of soft, vulnerable, protective look of who she was as a teenager." The layered, thrift-shop look of grunge — flannel shirts, vintage cardigans, ripped jeans — was originally nothing more than a practical response to the Pacific Northwest's temperamental climate (*MSCL* was filmed in southern California, but takes place in Pennsylvania), though it also combatted the flashy '80s aesthetic. For similar reasons, *MSCL*'s cast members were given their own closets from which to pick a finite number of items. "What happens with Hollywood TV shows is there's always a new change per episode — sometimes four or five — and they don't repeat stuff," Norris said. "I think that's why everyone looks so 'dressed' on TV now." Angela conversely wears her mustard plaid shirt, floral velvet dress, and green-sleeved sweater over and over and over again.

A staple of Angela's wardrobe are her Doc Martens, which were chosen for their trendiness but had an inadvertently feminist effect. In her essay "Chicks Goin' at It," Anastasia Higginbotham described how boots empowered her by changing the way she walked. "I no longer wobbled. I took bigger steps, surer steps, harder steps," she wrote. "It's clear to me now that every feminist, indeed every woman, needs a good, solid pair of boots. It's not just a symbolic assault on the patriarchy, it's a fashion statement." Angela's choice to bequeath the new green boots she gets for Christmas to Juliana Hatfield's homeless girl[6] thus has a dual meaning: it represents the similarity between the characters but also the passing of a totem of power from the more privileged wearer to the other. Angela's overalls, too, are symbolic, which is why she wears them when she is considering whether or not to sleep with Jordan Catalano. "You know, I'm a heterosexual male," Norris told *Refinery29*, "and my thinking was, you'd dress hot. But [Danes] came at it more from the angle that she wanted to protect herself."

As for the rest of the cast, Rickie's style came straight from the cover of The Beatles' 1967 art-rock album *Sgt. Pepper's Lonely*

---

6 At the time of her appearance on *MSCL*, singer-songwriter Juliana Hatfield was also something of a feminist icon for teen girls, thanks to her little-girl voice clashing with her big-girl lyrics. Like the third wave's riot grrrls, Hatfield used her music to combat oppression.

*Hearts Club Band*, with some Michael Jackson and Sal Mineo mixed in.[7] His best friend's look was also based on vintage stars. "I wanted Rayanne to be my kind of Janis Joplin, or a wild-child Cyndi Lauper," Norris told *Refinery29*. "I would mix stuff from period costume houses, thrift stores, and designer labels — you never had one designer on her — there was probably four or five different ones at any given time." Conversely, Sharon, a more conventional character, was clothed in department-store duds. "Sharon, to me, is someone who shops with her mom," Norris told *Vulture*. Brian gave off the same impression in his cords and button-down shirts (observing the shoulder bag constricting his chest in one scene, actor Devon Gummersall said on *The Complete Series*, "When you put on the clothes, it so informs your behavior.") But Jared Leto was the easiest to dress, in a simple flannel shirt and jeans. "It was almost like his uniform," Norris said. This was a subtle hint at Jordan Catalano's underprivileged background, which did not give him the means to change (either because he didn't have the money, or because he didn't have a closet). At one point, Angela notices his flannel top unravelling at the collar, "like he was from a poor family and couldn't afford a new shirt." Leto, who wore his own necklace throughout the series, also reminded Norris of Cobain, which gave him an unspoken sartorial connection to Angela.

The same way the characters' clothes spoke to their identities, mixing them symbolized the intermingling of those

---

7 The bisexual *Rebel Without a Cause* star actually gets a shout-out on *MSCL* in "So-Called Angels." "Maybe he's coming in late," Rayanne says when Rickie fails to show up to school. "Maybe he's at some Sal Mineo film festival." *Rebel Without a Cause*'s gay subtext, Mineo's character longing for Dean's, mirrors Rickie longing for Jordan.

identities. "The bonus for me is when they decided to have Claire dye her hair red," Norris told *Vulture*. "That was the key to finding the new look and trying to let her fit in more into Rayanne and Rickie's world." Marking the beginning of her metamorphosis from wallflower to woman, Angela's red hair was also the start of her transition from faint plaid to bold flannels, in which she dropped her conservative past for a grungier future ("You know, with your hair like that?" Rayanne says in the pilot. "It hurts to look at you."). In *Dear Angela*, Susan Murray writes that dressing like one's friends expresses solidarity and bonding. So we see Angela in a long black vintage dress with lace sleeves when she is mourning her relationship with Jordan (Norris: "That was absolutely the influence of Rayanne") and then sporting a harlequin-style shirt under her overalls, which is all Rickie, followed by a puffy vest with a shearling collar ("Very Jordan," says Norris). Then there's the Angela-esque plaid vest that Sharon breaks out in "Strangers in the House" when she's staying with her ex–best friend, the one person she wishes would comfort her when her father is sent to hospital. As Deidre Dowling Price explains in the *Dear Angela* essay "Whatever Happens Happens," "People pretend to be unlike themselves to temporarily exhibit characteristics they envy in others."

In *MSCL*'s first episode, Brian, forever an unwanted reminder of Angela's former life, chides Angela when she sneaks off to Let's Bolt on a school night in Rayanne's club clothes. "You're not stupid, don't act like it. It's a stupid act," he says. Angela replies coolly: "Everybody's an act. Including you." Act or no, Brian behaves consistently where Angela exercises her right not to, in order to determine who she actually is. She is stubborn and dismissive with her parents, but loses confidence with Jordan. She pulls rank with Danielle and Brian, but is pressured by Rayanne. And sometimes her various acts clash. "What I, like, dread is when people who know you in completely different ways end up in the same area," she says in "Dancing in the Dark," in the rare presence of Brian, Rayanne, and Rickie. "You have to develop, like, this combination you on the spot." This performative behavior speaks to the complexity and sometimes contradictory nature of teen identity.

Angela likes Halloween for this very reason. As she explains, "It's your one chance all year to be someone else." And though she doesn't initially wear a costume on the day in question — she ends up in Rayanne's aunt's clothes from the '60s — she already looks like someone else in a feminine, formfitting red dress and lipstick. "I should be wearing a costume, but who would I be?" she asks, before becoming a historical version of herself, because Angela is nothing if not solipsistic. (On her first date with Jordan, in "Why Jordan Can't Read," she curls her hair and wears a crocheted dress and bright pout. "You just look like you're going to a costume party as someone else," Brian says. But that someone else is simply an older version of her; note the crochet in the pilot.) And on Halloween night, she behaves appropriately unlike herself. "You could screw up your whole life," Brian says prior to her breaking into Liberty High with Rayanne, to which Angela responds, "At least I'll know I'm alive." Everyone else, in the meantime, settles into more conventional costumes. Patty and Graham reverse their regular roles by dressing up as Rapunzel and a pirate, respectively. It is while role-playing — Patty is temporarily submissive, Graham dominant — that they settle into a traditional gender dynamic, which frees them of their daily concerns about their unconventional domestic roles and allows them to have an explosive, if orthodox, sexual encounter. Similarly, Rickie scrubs himself of everything that makes him stick out in order to become Brian. "I thought this Halloween I'd be, you know, everyone else," he says. Then, of course, there's the morphing of Angela into Rayanne and Rayanne into Angela in "Betrayal."

Since appearance is connected to identity, it can similarly be challenged and performed. This causes notions of beauty to be equally expanded — making room for anyone and everyone as opposed to a chosen few. The decision to wear each other's clothes, as well as denoting our desire to try on others' identities, speaks to what we find beautiful regardless of whether it is so considered by others. This layers, so to speak, *MSCL*'s wardrobe, presenting it as a counterpoint to contemporary shows like *90210*, which served as glorified advertorials for a variety of clothing brands. These shows removed the subtle authenticity of the teen dressing experience, while the characters in *MSCL* inspired not only each other, but the fans watching them, who expressed sartorially their bond with them. "Their hair dyeing and choices of clothes help them bring what they have experienced through *MSCL* and their online community back into their everyday lives," Murray wrote in *Dear Angela*, noting that the internet acted as a sort of virtual bedroom, "a private space where girls can safely create their own subculture." One where they could feel free to try on different identities of their own, choosing and discarding aspects of Angela and her friends in order to figure out who they themselves were.

# 3

## That Rude Girl

"Go, now, go!" It's the first voice you hear, the first thing at all, really, in the opening of *My So-Called Life*. Three disembodied words over a black screen, and they aren't even spoken by the main character. Instead, it's Rayanne Graff, looking much older than her 15 years — dark lips, chandelier earrings, off-the-shoulder shirt — who is egging on a fresh-faced, crochet-topped Angela Chase to ask strangers for change. From the pilot on, Rayanne's encouragement is the first thing you hear at the top of each show, kicking off the theme song. Because as important as Angela is to *MSCL*, her transformation is even more so. And the agent of that change is Rayanne Graff.

"So, I started hanging out with Rayanne Graff," Angela's voice-over begins. "Just for fun, just 'cause it seemed like if I didn't, I would die, or something. Things were getting to me,

31

just how people are, how they always expect you to be a certain way, even your best friend." That would be Sharon Cherski, Angela's BFF from childhood, who has essentially been passed down through blood (she is the daughter of Angela's mom's best friend, Camille). On the surface, Sharon is the opposite of Rayanne, as "perfect" as Rayanne is "imperfect." Her grades are pristine, her looks are pristine . . . she even acts pristine, volunteering to help the less fortunate, dating the football star, never skipping school. Where Sharon is too controlled, Rayanne is too unruly. "She just lives life right on that edge and you don't know if she's going to fall off," actress A.J. Langer said of her character in *The Complete Series*. Rayanne drinks excessively, talks excessively, eats excessively — her guidance counselor calls her "orally fixated" — she dresses outrageously, moves constantly, and has sex even more than that. She has no father, barely a mother, and can only afford hand-me-downs, but in the first episode, Angela, standing next to Sharon, watches wistfully as Rayanne runs off school grounds with her best friend, Rickie Vasquez. Freedom.

Rayanne encourages Angela to change not only her hair, but everything beneath it as well. And by replacing Sharon with Rayanne, Angela flips that hair in the face of societal expectations. To be a feminist is to "join in sisterhood with women when often we are divided," wrote Rebecca Walker. Despite being separated by socioeconomic circumstances, Angela and Rayanne have found each other in the halls of Liberty High, where Rayanne doles out advice and Angela takes it. *MSCL* is one of the rare shows to centralize a character like this, humanizing the superficial "slut" stereotype. Rayanne enables the viewer to see beyond Angela's (and potentially his or her own) limited view, in which she is at the top of the hierarchy and Rayanne is at the bottom. Because to Angela, Rayanne's voice only matters by virtue of how it forms her own. "As we have listened for centuries to the voices of men and the theories of development that their experience informs, so we have come more recently to notice not only the silence of women but the difficulty in hearing what they say when they speak," Carol Gilligan wrote in 1982's *In a Different Voice*. "The failure to see the different reality of women's lives and to hear the differences in their voices stems in part from the assumption that there is a single mode of social experience and interpretation." For Angela, that mode is her own.

Unlike Angela's (or Sharon's) picket-fence provenance, Rayanne comes from a crystal ball of hippie-dippie smoke and mirrors, which she shares with a beautiful blond mystic. Amber Vallon is a countercultural single mom who works by night as an x-ray technician and feeds her daughter appetizers by day. She is a proponent of tarot, the Grateful Dead, and Kurt Vonnegut, i.e., she's staunchly anti-authority, something one does not expect from an authority figure. "From Hester Prynne in *The Scarlett Letter* to *Murphy Brown* in the TV sitcom, single mothers have been characterized and treated as immoral, a threat to society and essentially outcasts," writes Amelia Richards in her *Listen Up* essay "The Immaculate Conception." Amber easily claims Angela's affection because she's everything Patty is not (the same way Graham easily claims Rayanne's affection because he's everything Amber is not). She is emotive and open minded and basically a teenager herself, staying out until all hours, partying and sleeping in, unlike Patty and Graham, who maintain parental responsibility amid their struggles. In the pilot, Patty jokes about surveilling her daughter — "God, Chelsea Clinton. Will you look at this? No freedom, no privacy, constant surveillance, Secret Service men. That's what we need." — yet she is the one Angela (not to mention Rayanne and everyone else) runs to when she needs a parent. From where Angela stands, Amber's low-class life, and Rayanne's by extension, can be a lot of fun but is ultimately a lesson in irresponsibility, a sugar-rimmed prop supporting the Chases' upper-middle-class superiority.

"At Rayanne's, no one was home," Angela says in the pilot, watching her drunken friend being escorted by a cop up the steps to her dark apartment building (the Chases' glowing abode in the next scene offers a stark contrast). Despite her occasional charm, Amber is seen by the Chases as a neglectful parent and Rayanne as the frenzied product of her tetherless home life (as she struggles with sobriety in "On the Wagon," her mother coolly sips a daiquiri). Rayanne is on a perpetual quest to satiate herself (with no end in sight), and toward the end of the series, in "The Weekend," she explains why: "When I look at myself, I see everything in, like, slow motion and I think: 'Something has to happen.' Only it never does, so I have to make it happen." (This recalls her Godotian friend Tino, who never shows up. "Why would I want him to show up?" Holzman asks. "He was a wonderful device and a wonderful

34

fun way to have plots change and unfold.") Rayanne's life is so full of holes — absentee mom, absentee dad, no siblings, no Tino — that she is constantly trying to fill them with drink, drugs, and sex. But, Rayanne, who is so poor she can't even afford Christmas presents, lacks the privilege and therefore the access to the support network, including privileged friends — we're looking at you, Angela — required to shift herself beyond her prescribed role. Despite her heroic attempts to substitute lollies for liquor and occupy herself with theater work, to the Chases, in particular, Rayanne is forever operating within the narrative of the substance-abusing promiscuous product of a broken home who skips class, stays out late, and is constantly getting into trouble. "I can take care of myself!" she yells at her best friend after narrowly avoiding an assault, but it rings as false to Angela as Amber's declaration to Patty that she's "a damn good mother," when Patty stops by to check up on Rayanne in "On the Wagon." From the Chases' middle-class POV, their voices are as empty as each other, which says more about the limits of the Chases' reality than it does about Rayanne and her mother.

Because Rayanne's energy cannot be denied, her refusal to sit still sweeps Angela into action as well — Angela may not want to be Rayanne, but she idolizes her rebellion. Rayanne invites Angela to various events outside her suburban enclave — a club called Let's Bolt, a mosh-pitted party, Rayanne's own apartment — in order to land Angela her holy grail, Jordan Catalano. And by following Rayanne's lead, Angela goes from a place of security to a place of breaking and entering. And

Rayanne holds her hand through it all — emotionally as well as physically — incessantly imparting sage advice (if only she could talk to herself like this). In "The Zit," for instance, Angela finds out Sharon met her new boyfriend at a pep rally. "Should we be, like, attending those things?" she asks, to which Rayanne replies, "Please, grip yourself." Masquerading as a glib comment, this serves as Rayanne's affirmation of Angela's quest for her own identity. Grip yourself, not the person you think you should be.

Who Rayanne wants to be is clear from the start. As her mom says in "Guns and Gossip," "She wants to *be* Angela." This isn't garden-variety BFF envy: Rayanne's desire is less to become Angela herself and more to have her life and what it means — stability. To be Angela is to be in a world of nuclear families, where Brian Krakow crams for extra credit and Sharon Cherski catwalks for charity. As Michele Byers wrote in her introduction to *Dear Angela*, *MSCL* "seemed to signal a romantic (if not romanticized) longing for the safe serenity of a type of middle-class, suburban life in America." If not a longing for everyone, it certainly is for Rayanne — and Brian, at Christmastime, and Rickie, after being kicked out — who jokes that Angela takes for granted that she is "the product of a two-parent household" and has "the type of dad that would lay two Dead tickets on you." Not to mention Angela's mom, Patty, having the power to bring back the dead (she resuscitates an overdosing Rayanne in "Other People's Mothers"). From this privileged position, Angela feels free to pass judgment — no matter how petty or false — on everyone who lacks her advantages, while Rayanne doesn't have the means. (Sharon accuses her in the pilot of using Joanie Barsh, but she does not generally snub people like Angela does.) It's why — after a disastrous public performance with Jordan Catalano's band, right before she takes her first post-rehab sip in "On the Wagon" — Rayanne slips into a jazzy rendition of "Can You Tell Me How to Get to Sesame Street?" It's the musical narration of her inability to get to that mythical sunlit, cloudless place inhabited by the Angela in her mind.

In *MSCL*, the gates of suburbia are guarded by Patty "Cerberus" Chase, and she is immediately wary of "this Rayanne": "I don't think that she's the right friend for you," she tells Angela in "Other People's Mothers." Even Rayanne herself thinks she is unworthy of Angela's friendship, often citing her own promiscuity as a deal breaker. Remember it's Angela who claims to have approached Rayanne — "So I started hanging out with . . ." — not the other way around, so it's Angela who, once again, has the power. Rayanne feels threatened by Sharon's presence because she sees her not only as the member of an opposing preppie clique, but as someone who is as flawless as Angela ("she's not a slut"), and thus more worthy of her friendship. She is forever waiting for Angela to return to her senses and reunite with Sharon (which she eventually does, though in a sense this is a self-fulfilling prophecy because Rayanne's betrayal incites the event). For the same reason, Rayanne doesn't consider Sharon a friend even though they often confide in each other.

Though Rayanne's protective sentiment toward Angela smacks of irony — "I'll always watch out for you, 'kay," she says, drunkenly, in the pilot. "I'll always be there for you, so, don't worry, 'kay?" — she frequently tries to protect her best friend's innocence, which is the only other way (besides doling out advice) for Rayanne to claim power in their relationship. She is the weathered defender protecting the innocent maiden from the likes of Jordan Catalano. "You know you like her. Would it kill you to admit it? Maybe treat her halfway decent?" she tells him in the "Self-Esteem" episode. Before that, in "Guns and Gossip," when rumors start circulating that Jordan and Angela had "complete sex" in Jordan's car (they didn't), an intimidating Rayanne confronts him with, "You're not talking it up like some low-life derelict cretin telling everyone you did her, are you?" In another "Self-Esteem" scene, Angela is shocked to find her ex–best friend and her new best friend discussing her relationship. "The only reason we talk like this is because we care about you," Rayanne explains. Even in her own life, Rayanne is less important than Angela.

Because the Chases believe they are the ones with the exemplary lives, they assume they can save Rayanne (Rickie doesn't have much luck). In the pilot, Angela rescues a tipsy Rayanne from an assault by grabbing the perpetrator and yelling, "Let go of her!" And Patty is the one to resuscitate her daughter's best friend when she overdoses in "Other People's Mothers." Following this incident, Amber explains to Patty that they are part of the same "karass," "a group of people who kind of get mixed up in each other's lives in order to do God's will." It's just that God's will, as we see it through Angela's eyes, seems to tip entirely in the Chases' favor. "All over school, there are these certain places that are reserved for certain people," Angela says. "You're not supposed to cross certain lines." But she does it all the time, and so does her mother. It's Rayanne who has to stay on her side and is chased out of the Chase space.

But even though Angela trespasses to establish her own identity, she always returns home. The stability, the control she finds in her suburban life, and what that life promises, is what makes her go to class even when Rayanne and Rickie don't. Predictably, Angela's friendship with Rayanne starts to fray when the latter disrupts this cocoon. In "On the Wagon," Angela tries to explain to her mom the sudden distance she feels from Rayanne — she is vacillating over whether to attend her friend's first gig with Jordan's band — following Rayanne's almost-OD: "it's there, and it's been there for, like, a while, since that night when you had to drive her to the hospital. It's this thing that we never talk about." The "thing" is Rayanne's instability, the opposite of the thing that defines Angela — this is the invisible line that separates them. And Rayanne is aware of it. She's even primed for it, having always thought Angela was too good for her. "I just can't stand knowing what you're thinking about me," she tells Angela. "That I'm too messed up for you to be my friend anymore." At the end of the series, following the night that Rayanne sleeps with Jordan Catalano, Angela is back where she started, in familiar territory by Sharon's side. Though *MSCL* was not designed to end here, as it stands, the series implies that Rayanne has served her purpose: she has inspired Angela to change (somewhat) and act (she has finally communicated with Jordan Catalano). As for acquiring her own agency, for that, for hurting her friend — the very thing she said she would always protect Angela from — in order to claim, for a moment, her friend's life, Rayanne is punished.

Their friendship falters around the time Rayanne is cast in the school's production of Thornton Wilder's *Our Town* (Holzman's favorite play). In "Betrayal," she wins the main role of Emily Webb, a ghost who returns from the dead to relive her 12th birthday, only to realize how much she overlooked her life as she lived it. In this way, she parallels Rayanne, who is always searching for something more ("She is just now realizing how precious every moment of that life really was. And that she never really appreciated what she had," Mr. Katimski coaches her. "Just imagine what that must feel like, Rayanne.") To land the role, Rayanne performs, like Danielle did on Halloween, as Angela, folding her body in on itself and softening her voice. "I became you," she tells her friend. "Emily's supposed to be sweet and innocent, so I just imitated you." As the episode progresses, Rayanne and Angela appear to switch identities. Rayanne becomes quieter, her hair straighter, her accessories diminished. At one point, she even wears overalls. It's in the midst of this transformation into her best friend that she has sex with Jordan. Meanwhile, Angela becomes Rayanne as a means of seducing Corey Halfrick (who, ironically, has a crush on Rayanne). With her hair in braids, her lips red, Angela pounces on him and even asks for a drink. That Rayanne is lauded for her turn as Emily while Angela is criticized for playing Rayanne — regardless of how seamless the former's role-playing is on stage and how clunky the latter's is off it — is just another indication of which of them has more value.

"She's always partly wanted to be you," Rickie tells Angela in "Betrayal" after they discover Rayanne has slept with Jordan. "And in a way, I think this was her screwed up way of, for one night, kind of pretending she was you." It's fitting then that Brian Krakow, a persistent symbol of Angela's old life (before she claimed her independence), would precipitate the deterioration of her relationship with Rayanne. The yearbook videographer "happens" to record Rayanne's sexual encounter with Jordan and then delivers it to Sharon. "Is it being more of a friend to tell her or not tell her?" Sharon asks. Rhetorically, of course, because we know what she will decide — she's her mother's daughter, and Camille Cherski is the kind of person who warns her best friend that her husband might have a wandering eye. (Patty's response? "I love you. You are such a good friend.") To tell Angela is in Sharon's blood. "I said what I said to protect her, so she would know," she explains to Rayanne. "Because it's what you do when someone's your friend." But is it possible to have a true friendship when one friend is consistently fearful of not measuring up to the other's expectations? Rayanne idolizes Angela's stability, which by its very nature is unwavering. Angela idolizes Rayanne for her rebelliousness, yet expects her not to lose control. But isn't that the very nature of rebellion?

There's a reason Rayanne was pals with Rickie first. He is an outsider just as she is. Coming from the same social class, they know each other in a way Angela never can. Their bond precedes her; they are each other's family when no one else will be (not even the Chases). Rickie supports Rayanne when she drinks too much while Rayanne comes between Rickie and his bullies (she also chooses to respect the privacy he seems to want when he is left homeless, whereas Angela does not). As Bess Armstrong says in *The Complete Series* in reference to Sharon's disapproval of Rayanne, "Sharon could disapprove because she came from a stable family. Rickie didn't have the privilege." Neither did Jordan Catalano. But Angela did. And so did Winnie Holzman. "Rayanne's totally alone by her own making, and it reaches that level of heartbreak because Rayanne is somebody who knows that she created that for herself," she told *Vulture* of Rayanne's decision to have sex with Jordan. But didn't Angela place her on the pedestal from which she caused herself to fall so spectacularly? Considering how much she undervalues her position in their friendship, it follows that Rayanne would believe she is the one losing out when she finally talks to her best friend about her mistake. "You lost nothing, Angela. You lost a lousy selfish friend, a guy you never really had," she says. "You lost nothing! I lost a really good friend. I lost everything."

But considering all the ways Angela has failed to support Rayanne — she doesn't show up to her Embryos gig, she invites Rayanne over when she isn't home, she sells their Grateful Dead tickets — and Sharon — she drops her with no explanation and fails to console her when her father is in the hospital — calling Angela a "good friend" is as reductive as characterising Rayanne as a "bad" one. Their friendship is complicated, with good moments and bad moments, like anyone else's. "I would never have stopped exploring their relationship, but that's not the same as meaning they're kindred spirits," Holzman told *Vulture*. "It might have been they had more to do with each other, but not necessarily — and this is interesting to me — as friends." No, because a real friendship, a real sisterhood, means that you are both equal, on the same level despite your circumstances. In Angela's world, she is entitled to grow and change and make mistakes, but that privilege is hers alone.

# 4

## I Belong Nowhere

"Who taught you to hate the shape of your nose and the shape of your lips? Who taught you to hate yourself from the top of your head to the soles of your feet? Who taught you to hate your own kind?" Malcolm X delivered this speech in 1962. More than 30 years later, Angela Chase listens to it in a classroom at Liberty High. The words echo through the halls in "The Zit" only to re-form in "Self-Esteem" in the mouth of a teacher advising her friend Rickie Vasquez: "Nobody should hate who they are." But who is Rickie? He could be black, but he could also be Hispanic. He dresses like a guy, but he also wears eyeliner. He seems to like guys, but is almost always with girls. He sticks out in the women's bathroom, but he's also out of place in the men's. "I belong nowhere, with no one," he says in "Life of Brian." "I don't fit."

The first time we see Rickie, he's skipping school with his best friend, Rayanne Graff. In his next scene, he smiles approvingly as Angela stares ambivalently at her newly dyed hair. Then, his first line, upon an awkward first encounter with Patty Chase: "You're Angela's mom? I like your house." Rickie is always there for the women. He generally serves to comment on discussions between Rayanne and Angela — "That is deep." "I completely understand this." "That does have the ring of truth." — acting as a modern-day Greek chorus. The external antidote to Angela's internal voice, he provides insight (like surmising for Angela why Rayanne slept with Jordan) and expresses what the main characters cannot (like telling Brian he is using Jordan to confess his feelings for Angela). "It was as if Rickie was the moral compass of the show," actor Wilson Cruz said in *The Complete Series*. For this reason, more than anyone else on the show, Rickie is beloved by fans. Like some kind of teen Mother Teresa, he is the embodiment of compassion. As his friends' personal rock, he is almost entirely selfless, almost entirely non-judgmental — his ability to maintain friendships with both Rayanne and Angela following Rayanne's betrayal is one of many examples of this — a feat at any time in life, but in adolescence, when solipsism is a virtual right, it is astonishing. His emotional intelligence goes far beyond that of his peers, not to mention most adults. (Angela should be asking him for advice as much as Rayanne.) Rickie is a loyal friend who demands nothing in return. What's not to love?

Despite offering the most mature advice and acting as the girls' mouthpiece — Rickie is the one who reads Angela's anonymous *Liberty Lit* story in class — he is often overlooked and taken for granted, in part because he is so focused on everyone else. "You just think of me as someone who's, you know, around," he says to Angela in "Guns and Gossip" when they find themselves in a rare moment of solitude early in their friendship. Rickie even sees himself that way. "I can see it from your side, but I also see it from her side and from my own side," he tells Angela of Rayanne in "Father Figures." "But I don't really have a side." Rickie does have a side — it's just harder to come by. "I wanted him to be hard to pin down," Winnie Holzman explained in *The Complete Series*. So she created a mixed-race character (on paper, he is half black, half Latino) whose gender and sexuality are ambiguous. "He wasn't clear where he stood or who he was, because he was 15 years old," Holzman explained in *Variety*. And he wasn't the only one. According to Holzman, ABC's Standards and Practices, the department responsible for checking up on *MSCL*'s morality, called her in confusion over a scene in the pilot in which Rickie applies eyeliner in the girls' bathroom. "What I learned is that what was perhaps scary about Rickie to the network was not that he was gay, but that I saw him as feminine," she said, adding, "That was a very specific kind of person, and it's almost a bigger taboo than being gay." Holzman broke stereotypes, so why not taboos?

Like Angela, Rickie is seeking his identity; it's just his job is a lot harder. Angela is all-around privileged — upper middle class, white, cis, hetero — which gives her the freedom to search for her own identity and be confident in the knowledge that she will be accepted no matter which one she chooses. But things are not so clear for Rickie. His home life is so unstable that at one point he doesn't even have one, removing the space to explore his race, gender, and sexuality, let alone his identity beyond that. He is deemed an outsider by virtue of his appearance (mixed race, feminine) and is constantly at the mercy of a white patriarchal society regardless of how he identifies. Actor Wilson Cruz was familiar with this liminal space in society, and it was this bias that he was intent on combatting by playing Rickie. "I wanted to say to young gay Latino men that we are valuable people and can fill our lives with quality experiences," he told *The Advocate* in 1999. "I want to be an example of that."

In 1994, a study released by the National Council of La Raza, a Latino civil rights group, revealed that the number of Latino characters on TV had dropped 2 percent since the '50s. (They were also more negatively represented than white or black characters.) *MSCL* was one of the rare series to represent people of color (though few graduate beyond background-performer status), not to mention the first prime-time show to feature a recurring gay teen. It was time, after all. By the early 1990s, the political and cultural landscapes were overrun by activists promoting the inclusion of diverse sexualities, races, and genders. Conservatives, meanwhile, held tight to "American values" — white, heterosexual, patriarchal — in opposition to the multiculturalism they believed was fracturing the once-united States. "Much of the era's gay-themed programming was fundamentally about being straight in an era when increased gay visibility and gay rights battles highlighted and challenged heterosexuality's ex-nominated privileges," Ron Becker wrote in *Gay TV and Straight America* (2006), adding, "I would also argue that much of the era's gay-themed programming reflected the ambivalence certain viewers likely felt about both multiculturalism and homosexuality." *MSCL* exposes this discomfort in "So-Called Angels" when Graham questions whether Patty would vacillate about helping Brian — who is straight and shares the Chases' socioeconomic status — if, like Rickie, he showed up at their house with a black eye.

While the first four decades of TV "virtually denied the existence of homosexuality," according to Becker, by the mid-to-late '90s, "40 percent of all primetime network series produced at least one gay-themed episode." And it was the creators of *MSCL*, Marshall Herskovitz and Ed Zwick, who propped open the closet. In 1989, a scene in their ABC series *thirtysomething* showed a post-coital gay couple in bed. For fear of alienating consumers, advertisers pulled out of the show and ABC lost $1.5 million, which was enough of a blow to keep them from rerunning the episode. A similar reaction greeted *L.A. Law* two years later after it aired a scene in which two women kissed — though no relationship developed between the characters. (As *Buffy the Vampire Slayer* writer Marti Noxon told NPR, regarding execs' resistance to a relationship between characters Willow and Tara, "You can show girls kissing once, but you can't show them kissing twice . . . because the second time, it means that they liked it.") But the LGBT rights movement was out and proud, and gay-themed episodes persisted

— with a catch. "Networks were greenlighting gay material as long as producers carefully avoided serious gay issues or images of same-sex intimacy," Becker wrote. So, the year before *MSCL*'s pilot aired, while two teen girls smooched in the dark in *Picket Fences*, *Seinfeld* introduced the PC meme "not that there's anything wrong with that."

Though *The Advocate* dubbed Wilson Cruz a "poster boy for gay youth" for playing Rickie Vasquez, his character was as chaste as every other gay role on TV. Rickie's crush on pretty boy Jordan Catalano precedes Angela's by a mile but is almost never acknowledged. Part of that is Jordan's alpha reputation for overt heterosexuality, but it's still jarring for neither Rayanne nor Angela to recognize Rickie's desire while incessantly indulging Angela's. Until you realize that, for Angela, sexuality is not an issue — heterosexuality has the Pope's blessing — so it barely occurs to her that it could be a problem for anyone else. Rickie's crush instead dissolves into the background along with him, despite how conspicuous it is to the viewer. "Don't you love how he leans?" he says in the pilot, voicing the words in Angela's head. Later, he is clearly begging for permission to engage with Jordan — "You want me to talk to him? Because I'm willing to do it!" — only to be ignored, the same way he is ignored by society at large. The difference here being that we see Angela not seeing him — *MSCL* forces us to acknowledge the prejudice that surrounds us and even engulfs our heroine. It's only when Rickie rattles off Jordan's schedule in "Why Jordan Can't Read" that Angela acknowledges Rickie's feelings, only to have him let her off with "You don't have to say it." In other words, his sexuality is unspeakable, even for him. Though Rickie matures as the series progresses, evidenced by his confrontation with Angela over her advances toward his second crush, Corey Halfrick — "Guess how I felt?" he asks her in "Betrayal" — he still only considers going with Corey to the school dance "in some imaginary universe that, like, exists in my mind."

In the actual universe, the perception at the time was that to be gay was to be sick. Wilson Cruz counted himself among a number of angry young gay men in the early '90s who were being discriminated against due to AIDS and conservativism. In the '80s, the spread of HIV was initially associated with the gay community. (AIDS, acquired immunodeficiency syndrome, was originally called GRID, gay-related immune deficiency.) Awareness increased in 1985 after closeted actor Rock Hudson became the first celebrity to die from AIDS, which had a major effect on the funding of AIDS research, and the Gay & Lesbian Alliance Against Defamation (GLAAD) formed to protest homophobic news reporting. But it wasn't until 1990 that the World Health Organization stopped labeling homosexuality an illness, and it was another four years before the American Medical Association did the same thing. In the meantime, Cruz used *MSCL* to subvert persistent gay stereotypes. "Winnie Holzman had a very open and nurturing relationship with all of us," he told *Vulture* in 2014. "She got to know about our lives, and a lot of that seeps into the storytelling."

RuPaul's motto — "My artistry is my activism" — was adopted by Cruz when *The Advocate* asked him about his choice to come out at the beginning of his career, describing it as "a feat every bit as revolutionary as an established star's coming out of the closet." In other words, he came out because his character did. "The whole point of that character was he was on this journey of self-acceptance," Cruz told *Entertainment Weekly*, "and if I wasn't on that journey as well, then I would be sending out the wrong message." And, like his character, when the actor announced to his father that he was gay, he was kicked out. Cruz's admission in the press that he had the same experience as Rickie resulted in him being "inundated" with letters from gay teens who claimed he had saved their lives. In 2005, Winnie Holzman's own daughter, Savannah Dooley, wrote in *The Advocate* about how Rickie enlightened her experience growing up as a lesbian. "Living in Los Angeles with two parents in show business, I knew what being gay meant from an early age," she wrote. "But seeing the character of Rickie helped shape my views about homosexuality." As she got older, Dooley started noticing the "badly written" gay characters on other shows, which were riddled with clichés. "I could appreciate more of the nuances of *MSCL*, like the fluidity of Rickie's sexual and gender expression," she wrote in *TIME* for the show's 20th anniversary. "He starts out identifying as bi before eventually coming out as gay; he wears makeup but experiments with a traditionally masculine look on Halloween; he tries using both the girls' and the boys' bathroom at school but doesn't quite fit in either. These details felt authentic to me as a teenage queer in flux, trying on different labels to find what felt right. It reassured me to know not everyone's journey began with 'I always knew.'"

*MSCL*'s Christmas episode, in which Rickie is kicked out of his home for coming out, stands out not only for being the one time his character eclipses Angela, but for being the only one which excludes credits, theme song, and voice-over. "For the grace of God go I" is the theme, and Angela recognizes that her class, her race, her sexuality, and her privilege separate her reality from her friend's. As Juliana Hatfield's homeless character (angel?) puts it, "Another toss of the dice, I could be in her shoes, she could be in mine." This is the truth, it is inarguable, so Angela's subjective voice-over has no place here. But what about Rickie's? Holzman says that she wasn't trying to make "a statement" by giving him a major story but no interior monologue. "It never came up as a thought to have him narrate," she says via email. "We just wrote it and that's how it came out." While this would seem to defy the show's intention to shatter stereotypes — he is not afforded a voice to the same extent as Angela — the episode is as much about Angela realizing how different she is from Rickie as it is about Rickie himself. Considering *MSCL* focuses primarily on Angela's life, it corresponds that those with lives more like hers — Brian and Danielle — would be afforded voice-overs and not Rickie (or Rayanne for that matter). "We're not creating a symbol for the gay community," Cruz told the *Dallas Morning News* in 1994. "We're just saying this is part of Angela's life, just like it's a part of a lot of people's lives." The intention was not so much to wave a rainbow flag as it was to thread Rickie's sexuality through the show's tapestry.

Perhaps that's why Rickie so often seems like an afterthought — because to Angela, in all her privilege, he is. In *The*

*Complete Series*, *MSCL*'s producers confessed that Rickie's story-line in the World Happiness Dance episode ("Life of Brian") — he pines for Corey Halfrick, who pines for Rayanne Graff — only developed because actress A.J. Langer was sick. Neither did Holzman plan on Rickie admitting he was gay until she explored it through another white cis hetero character, Delia Fisher. "First, I really related to Delia, and her having a crush on him and everything. So, her being very attracted to him and him being attracted to the idea of her, like, 'Wow, could I, like, have a girlfriend and go that whole route? Could I pull that off?' made sense to me," Holzman told *Vulture*. "And his realization that he couldn't, I think, had to do with, in a funny way, his affection for her. 'This girl really likes me. She's around me all the time. I really like her too. She's a sweet person. She's a good person. I even think she's cute. But it's like . . . I'm so gay.' It was almost like a come-to-Jesus moment for him."

When Rickie eventually accepts the "gay" descriptor — Cruz has said the term's rare appearance on the show reflected his own high-school experience — he is actually considering dating Delia. "Do you realize how much easier my life would be if I could just like her back?" he tells Brian. "This could be my chance to be straight." But in the end Rickie is not as invisible as Angela makes him out to be:

*Delia:*
*You're gay, right?*

*Rickie:*

*Well, I, uh, you know.*

*Delia:*

*That came out so rude.*

*Rickie:*

*No, see I try not to, um, no, I don't like, uh. Yeah. I'm gay. I just don't usually say it like that.*

*Delia:*

*How do you usually say it?*

*Rickie:*

*I don't usually say it. I mean, I've actually never said it . . . out loud.*

It makes sense that the catalyst for Rickie's admission would be the girl who dreamed about dancing with him in a vegetable garden. For Rickie, the dance floor — that dreamy lacuna outside the quotidian clunk of real life — is the only place he feels free, the same way it was for Cruz. "The thing about me and school was that as much as I felt that I didn't belong, as long as I was on a stage or dancing, that's where I excelled the most, felt worthy," he told *Entertainment Weekly* in 2007. "So that episode, where he takes off and just doesn't give a damn about anything was a celebration. Completely liberating." In the scene in question, both he and Delia — recently jilted by Brian — are tapping their feet to Haddaway's "What Is Love?" on the sidelines of the World Happiness Dance. After shyly sizing each other up, Rickie motions to the dance floor and Delia accepts his invitation. The duo tentatively starts to dance, falling in step with the crowd, becoming part of it. Then, abruptly, Rickie breaks free. He throws his arms in the air, thrusts his pelvis, spins around. Delia pauses, initially shocked, but, slowly, takes his lead. The other students form a circle around them as they dominate the center of the room. Everyone is riveted. And at the end of the song, the entire crowd erupts as Rickie and Delia fall into each other's arms.

The scene is, in effect, the answer to Haddaway's question. It's a moment of solidarity — a moment in which Rickie's flamboyance is rewarded rather than maligned — that you would never expect Rickie to experience. As he tells Angela in "The Zit," "You blend in, unlike, say, me, who basically never will." Like Rayanne, he envies Angela's ability to embody traditional American values. "I would give anything to have your life," he says in "Guns and Gossip." "You have this great house, parents who are, like, there, and no one bothers you at school." Yet when he does end up living in that world, he is unable to blend in, as he predicted. "I find Rickie a little confusing," Angela's mom says in the pilot. When her daughter explains that "maybe he's bi," she gets even more confused: "How can he be bi anything? He's a child; he's obviously very confused." Patty understands Jordan's sex life — and it's unlikely just because he's two years older than Rickie — so her comment about Rickie seems to speak to her generation's association of homosexuality with AIDS (hence the implication that bisexuality requires adult responsibility). Similarly, though Patty admits to being in the same karass as Rayanne, when she is faced with Rickie's bruises, she argues that it's not her place to get involved. "I think he does make you kind of uncomfortable," Graham says in "So-Called Angels." "What if that was Brian Krakow with that bruise on his face? That would be a different story, wouldn't it?" As aforementioned, here *MSCL* enables us to question our own potential ambivalence about homosexuality and multiculturalism through Patty's ambivalence about those very same things.

Ironically, Patty has much more in common with Rickie than she does with either Brian or Rayanne. They are both adopted, both have abandonment issues, both are pristinely clean, both know who Mary Quant is. So in "So-Called Angels," when Rickie rushes into Patty's arms and whispers, "Mom," it sounds natural. It is equally natural for Rickie to consider her more of a parent than, say, Rayanne's mom, or even his own relatives. He would have intuited that the perfect home in the '90s was the classic intact, middle-class family. Juliana Hatfield specifically composed the song "Make It Home," according to Cruz an inverted melody of the Christmas carol "Silent Night," for the Christmas episode, and it acts as the theme that pushes Rickie and the Chases together. At the end of the episode, when Rickie hugs Patty, a choir (Inner Voices) serenades them with "I Feel Like Going Home."

Still, Rickie, like Rayanne, is sometimes more a project than a person to Angela and her mom. As Jes Battis writes in the

*Dear Angela* essay "My So-Called Queer: Rickie Vasquez and the Performance of Teen Exile," "Rickie is the homeless, rootless character surrounded by comfortably domiciled and self-knowing people who want nothing more than to figure him out, to straighten him out, to fix him." When Rickie briefly stays with the Chases after being kicked out of his home, Graham and Patty discover his "incredible" talent for domesticity. "We should adopt," Graham quips, to which Patty replies, "If only it were that easy." Patty's daughter seems to have taken after her in this way. At one point, Angela even refers to Rickie as her possession. "She dreamed about Rickie? My Rickie?" she says in "In Dreams Begin Responsibilities" after hearing Delia did just that. Being another one of Rickie's white saviors, fetching him at a flop house and pressuring her family to share their home with him, is her attempt at changing the world, no matter how misguided it may be. ("Instead of changing the world, people sit in class and write notes about other people," she says in "Guns and Gossip." "It's like sometimes people fill their minds with all these stupid things to keep themselves from thinking about what's really important.") As Rayanne puts it in "So-Called Angels," in reference to Rickie, "Angela, you can't, like, be responsible for the whole world."

Rickie's failure to embody the Chases' ideal of the white upper-middle-class nuclear family actually makes him more dissatisfied with his own life than he might otherwise be. "They're this really great family, but in a way that made me feel lonelier," he tells Mr. Katimski, the English teacher who eventually takes him in in "Resolutions." It's not that Mr.

Katimski's family is inferior to the Chases; it's that they can relate to Rickie's experience. Mr. Katimski and his gay partner are forced to keep their sexuality a secret to avoid being ostracized at school, and they provide role models that align with Rickie's sexuality. (Though Rickie's friends accept him, they don't understand him the way Katimski does.) Rickie's New Year's resolution is "to find some place where I, like, really belong," and in a sense he does. And within his own safe space, he finally has the chance to explore his identity in the same way that Angela explores hers. And Wilson Cruz his. In 2013, then a national spokesperson and strategic giving officer at GLAAD, the actor wrote an essay for NBC Latino called "What Am I?" which answered the questions posed when we first saw him on *My So-Called Life*. "I am a Puerto Rican gay man. That is how I identify. That is my identity," he wrote. "I say Puerto Rican first because it is the obvious. It's written all over my face. I say I am gay after I say I am Puerto Rican because without learning to be proud of my 'Rican-ness' and the strength I gained from that pride, I wouldn't have had the strength to share with you that I am a gay man."

# 5

## How to Be a Man

On paper, Brian Krakow and Jordan Catalano are opposites
— Brian is the geeky good kid with the big hair, Jordan is
the soulful bad boy with the dreamy lean — but neither of
them can stick to script. Brian is a lot stronger than his stereotype would have you believe while Jordan is a lot more sensi-
tive. This constant tension between who these guys are and
who they've been told to be confounds them both. As Angela
Chase's father puts it, "Boys your age can sometimes not know
how to be what you want them to be."

If the '80s were for men, the '90s were for women; this
was the decade that brought us commodified Girl Power in
the form of the Spice Girls. "To be a heterosexual male in
the 1990s did not necessarily imply the conventionality that
it implied in the 1980s," explained Nicholas Birns in the *Dear*

*Angela* essay "Jordan Catalano/Brain Krakow: Masculinity, the 'Alternative' '90s, and *My So-Called Life*." Together, Brian, Jordan, and Rickie embody postmodern masculinity's botched attempt at breaking away from male gender norms. Brian and Jordan, in particular, nod to the two traditional masculine extremes — soft and hard, respectively — though they fail to fully realize them. Meanwhile, Rickie Vasquez's gender is ostensibly masculine, yet he engages in feminine-coded behavior — applying makeup, hanging out with girls in the girls' bathroom. When Rayanne informs him in "The Zit" that another student asked if he wanted a sex change, he responds, "I don't want to be a girl. I just want to hang with girls. There's a difference." Rayanne already knows that. It's something she acknowledges by asking Rickie for "the male perspective" while he touches up his eyeliner. "The great thing about being gay is, we get to redefine what it is to be male, what it is to be female, and the nature of relationships," actor Wilson Cruz told *The Advocate* in 1999. "So when we want to conform to the notions of gender and relationships inherited from straight people, we're missing the opportunity to help them and society by challenging those definitions."

The definitions *were* slowly being challenged and with them, Hollywood. As Winnie Holzman noted in an interview with *Variety*, the year the *MSCL* pilot was shot (1993), Neil Jordan's *The Crying Game* won an Oscar. The film was controversial at the time for presenting a main character, played by Stephen Rea, in a relationship with a trans woman, played by androgynous actor Jaye Davidson (who became the first mixed-race Brit nominated for an Oscar). In an interesting side note, Davidson confessed to the *Seattle Times* that year that his effeminacy was not actually considered "attractive" by the gay community ("To be homosexual is to like the ideal of the sex," he said, conjuring images of Rickie gazing longingly at Jordan). Then there was Michael Jackson's *Oprah* interview. Ninety million people reportedly tuned into the King of Pop's first on-screen interview in 14 years, in which he appeared with long, wavy black hair, sculpted eyebrows, pearl eyeshadow, chunky eyeliner, red lips, and white foundation. He then proceeded to drop the bomb that he had vitiligo and complained about how people perceived his appearance — it was the male gaze coming face to face with itself.

In one of the first scenes in *MSCL*, Angela complains about this male gaze. "Like with boys, how they have it so easy," she says. "How you have to pretend that you don't notice them . . . noticing you." The psychological concept of the gaze, in which a subject loses agency upon becoming a visible object, dates back to 20th-century French psychoanalyst Jacques Lacan. But it was only acknowledged as the infamously gendered space it is recognized as today when British film theorist Laura Mulvey came along during the second wave and published the essay "Visual Pleasure and Narrative Cinema." "The determining male gaze projects its fantasy on to the female form which is styled accordingly," she wrote in *Screen* magazine in 1975. "Traditionally, the woman displayed has functioned on two levels: as erotic object for the characters within the screen story, and as erotic object for the spectator within the auditorium, with a shifting tension between the looks on either side of the screen." So the woman is dominated not only by the man on-screen, by virtue of being presented within the confines of a patriarchal ideology, but by the audience (both male and female) viewing her as well. Everyone around her image is thus subscribing to this inequity, the idea that the woman is nothing more than a passive object to be acted upon by man.

That's not really how it works in *MSCL*. The first time we see Jordan Catalano, he is leaning against a locker — "Don't you love how he leans?" — and shutting what appear to be drug-addled eyes. "I'm in love," Angela says. "His name is Jordan Catalano. He was let back, twice. Once I almost touched his shoulder in the middle of a pop quiz. He's always closing his eyes like it hurts to look at things." He may return later, untouchably cool — quoth Rayanne, "Jordan Catalano doesn't go to school dances as, like, policy" — but here he is presented via Angela's gaze: beautiful and vulnerable. Even his name, Jordan, skews feminine. And not unlike the "dumb blond" type, his beauty makes more of an impression than his brains. "Here's what he's like: fairly out of it. Not unintelligent. Sort of, um, stray puppy, you know the type you're always trying to ease their pain. He may even be a halfway decent person, but let me tell you — trouble. Way too gorgeous." This is how Hallie Lowenthal, Graham's chef school protégé, describes Jordan in "Pressure"; his pulchritude supersedes all else. Her description recalls Ed Zwick telling Claire Danes and Devon Odessa (a.k.a. Sharon Cherski), as he introduced the young actresses to Jared Leto, "Girls, look what I have for you." The avatar of male objectification, Jordan Catalano exists to be looked at. And that's what we did. Few of the girls who watched *MSCL* failed to comment on Jordan's appearance. Even his co-stars had trouble seeing beyond it. "It's hard not to talk about how beautiful he is," Danes told *People* in 1995. "We teased him on the set. We'd say, 'Well, another woman has gone gaga over you.' Or, 'Okay, we give up. You're the most beautiful person in the universe.' He must be really sick of it." According to Winnie Holzman, he was. "Jared was clearly not interested in kind of following the traditional path of somebody who was that physically attractive," she says. "It was clear that that wasn't how he saw himself or wasn't what he was interested in."

In 1975, Laura Mulvey didn't believe men could be objectified. At that point, they overwhelmingly controlled the film industry, and she concluded that "the male figure cannot bear the burden of sexual objectification." Four decades later, things were different. In an interview with *Ms.* magazine in 2014, *Transparent* creator Jill Soloway aligned herself with *Orange Is the New Black*'s Jenji Kohan and claimed they were responsible for "inventing the female gaze." But on the basis of her definition, Winnie Holzman may have been its real progenitor. "We're trying to show sex and desire from a female vantage point," Soloway said, adding, "it's all about subverting the male gaze and not allowing men to control the narrative." In the case of *MSCL*, Holzman wrote Jordan Catalano as an object of Angela's desire and chose Jared Leto to embody him. And even though it wasn't always a woman behind the camera

— only three female directors and three female writers (besides Holzman) were involved in *MSCL* — Jordan was still ultimately the creation of a woman, designed to interact with a central female character who basically controlled the proceedings. See, it's Angela's gaze, and the men are just objects in it. Jordan leans as though he were simply falling into position as erotic object, like a painter's model onto a divan.[8] Angela has the ultimate power in this relationship, not only because she's the one who looks — symbolically, Jordan always has his eyes shut — but because of everything else too. She's an intelligent, upper-middle-class virgin while Jordan is as underprivileged as Rickie. (In "So-Called Angels," the two of them bond over their shared history of homelessness and abuse.) In "Guns and Gossip," Angela's thoughts drown out Jordan's attempt to proposition her. Though he is ostensibly exerting his dominance, Jordan is diminished to a voiceless object like so many women before him. That a man has been reduced by a woman to the lowly position of the women preceding him implies a lateral move rather than a progressive one, but perhaps this was an essential detour on the path toward the creation of the female gaze.

Jared Leto was originally only meant to appear in the *MSCL* pilot; like the so-called ditzes before him, he had to prove he was more than just a pretty face. Informed by his own turbulent adolescence as a fatherless dropout, Leto imbued Jordan's tough persona with a certain delicacy. Like Leto, Jordan has to take care of himself; presenting himself as

---

8  The name "Jordan" in fact comes from the Hebrew word for "one who descends."

a roughneck is a de facto requirement. He never skips shop, has an almost intimate relationship with his car, and teases nerdy female teachers along with the rest of his friends. So when he angers Angela in "Why Jordan Can't Read," she uses his alpha male rep against him: "Was it too emotional, too personal, too many big words?" Yet Jordan also composes music (about his car, but still), is ashamed of his dyslexia, and protects the bullied (Rickie, in particular). As Jes Battis writes in *Dear Angela*, he "is capable of these quiet and compassionate moments, these breaches in the fabric of his own enforced masculinity." Jordan's dream job, for instance, is to make snow like "those guys up in the mountains," which has a distinctly Holden Caulfield–esque ring to it. ("I would have to cop to that," Holzman tells me. "There was a way in which I was thinking about Salinger, absolutely.") He is the romantic mountain man, more Edward Scissorhands than Paul Bunyan.

Jordan's complex relationship with his own sex translates into an equally fraught relationship with the opposite. He has been raised in a culture that encourages men to either seduce human Barbies like Casey Hall (Liberty High's Most Beautiful) or have meaningless sex with the likes of Rayanne Graff (Most Slut Potential). Even Angela is wary of asking him if he would ever consider a girl to front his band when Tino drops out of Frozen Embryos. He only begrudgingly accepts Rayanne when the drummer, her new make-out partner, suggests it. "We'll do OK," Jordan tells her before their first gig together, "just wear something tight." His experience does not account for a girl like Angela Chase. Like his quiet and compassionate moments, she breaches the fabric of his masculinity. "It's like you think you're safe, or something. 'Cause you can just walk away anytime. Because you don't, like, need her. You don't need anyone," he tells Angela's mom in "In Dreams Begin Responsibilities." "But the thing you didn't realize is . . . you're wrong." Going through the motions of the definitive male, he confines his relationships to its prescripts, whether or not he really wants to.

Jordan's relationship with Angela, like his relationship with himself, blows hot and cold. He alternately propositions her and tells her, "I don't have any real interest in you." He repeatedly makes out with her, then calls her a "nobody" to his friends. He invites her to a concert, then accuses her of crowding him. He hugs her, then lets go when his friends show up. He agrees to meet her parents, but then he doesn't come over. "Admit it first," Angela says in "Self-Esteem." "That all of this happened. That you have emotions." But he can't do that: it's not in his vocabulary. The closest Jordan comes to affection is to caution her in "Pressure," "Don't take your turns too wide or anything." But, to Angela, this is momentous, a move (no matter how minor) away from the role he has been prescribed, toward his own personhood. "Sometimes someone says something really small," she coos in voice-over, "and it just fits right into this empty place in your heart." That Jordan uses Brian Krakow in an attempt to progress further is actually a regression (both of them reverting to well-established roles), but for a guy who systematically cheats on his homework, it's not a surprise. Brian is the shortcut Jordan needs: he speaks Angela's language.

Angela grew up with Brian. Neighbors from equally privileged middle-class, two-parent households, both are the kind of kids who were born to never play hooky. Both hate dancing. Both have unrequited crushes ("I resolve to stop obsessing over Angela Chase," Brian says in "Resolutions"). After Angela sees the squat where a bunch of homeless kids live in "So-Called Angels," she says to Brian, "they're like us," acknowledging in that "us" that she and him are a unit, one and the same. Their similarities are highlighted in "Why Jordan Can't Read," when Angela lambastes Brian for calling Jordan an idiot. "You think you understand but you don't!" she yells. "You just analyze everything until it barely exists!" Then the two of them stare at each other; it's only a moment, but in that moment Angela appears to realize she is speaking to herself, that Brian Krakow is her. And what she hates in him, she hates in herself. In that avant-garde post-gender moment, their similarities transcend sex.

It is a testament to their proximity that Brian is the only other character besides Angela and her sister who is afforded a voice-over in *MSCL*. And in "Life of Brian," his interior monologue is virtually indistinguishable from Angela's. "There's something about my life, it's just automatically true that nothing actually happens," he says, and, "So maybe this is what people mean when they talk about, you know, life." He and Angela have the same deluded view of reality. When Angela is simply asking to tag along with him and his date to the school dance, he says (in voice-over), "When you stripped away all the blathering, Angela Chase was asking to go to the dance with me." When she calls him "heartless" for jilting his date, he says, also in voice-over, "How ironic can you get without, like, puking." What separates them is the fact that, for now anyway, Angela is rejecting the life they shared while Brian is not. Again, it's the girl who is active here, not the guy.

The first time we see Brian, he is being pummelled against a bunch of lockers in the pilot. In another scene, his cafeteria tray is being rammed against his chest. The rest of the time he's studying Angela (where Jordan has his eyes closed all the time, Brian always has his on her), when he's not actually studying. That Jordan at one point misreads his name as "Brain" is no accident. As Michele Byers writes in *Dear Angela*, "a pattern of Jewish stereotypes appears in the construction of Brian's character: he is a 'brain,' his parents are a psychologist and a psychiatrist, he is upper middle class, he is anxious and high-strung and uptight." And Brian's raison d'être is to maintain that status quo. "I don't condemn it but I don't condone it," he tells Sharon Cherski of the sexist sophomore girls top 40 poll in "The Zit." He'll observe, but he won't confront. "I became yearbook photographer because I liked the idea that I could sort of watch life without having to be a part of it," he explains in voice-over. But, like Angela, he doesn't always do what he says.

Brian is not simply a passive, spineless, pink-shirted geek in accelerated. As meek as he may look, he is still a guy, which affords him certain privileges that *MSCL*'s girls are not. In the pilot, a cop asks him to "watch out for" Angela when she arrives home late. (A perennial feminist issue is the fight to take ownership of one's own safety.) Then there's the montage of Brian answering every question in every class. "You just sit at the back and keep quiet and let the boys shout out the answers, which they will even if they're wrong," Angela later narrates in "Self-Esteem." "Boys are less afraid of being wrong." And, aside from the fact that he secretly listens to heavy metal, he also possesses a hidden core of dependability (fueled by obligation, but still) that not even Jordan in all his uber-masculinity can equal. "Do you, like, realize the pressure on a person when it's, like, assumed that they will always get As?" he asks Angela in "Self-Esteem." "You have the option of insanity. I do not." His persona remains fixed when no one else's does. Though he is threatened with expulsion in "Guns and Gossip," he stands up for Rickie when Rickie is involved in a school shooting; Brian's stomach trouble actually clears up the moment he gets involved, as though all he needed to become self actualized was a purpose. And when Sharon's jock boyfriend abandons her after her dad has a heart attack in "Strangers in the House," it's Brian who steps in to support her ("So, girl in distress throws herself on guy with no life, huh?" Rayanne snarks). Despite his inability to say no to Angela's frequent requests for help, however, he does stand up to her. But, of course, in confronting Angela, Brian has nothing to lose. Like her, he would be losing a person he "never really had" (in his case, Angela; in Angela's case, Jordan), but neither his popularity (he has none) nor his security (like Angela, his family is privileged) are reliant upon him maintaining his role.

Angela finds Brian "reassuring and annoying." He is the one standing next to her when she sees her dad talking to a woman who is not her mother. She hides in his car when she is avoiding her family. She wears his sweater when she is cold, asks him to stay when she needs company. She gets extra credit through him ("I pity you," Sharon tells Brian). And Brian's just happy to be around her. He watches her from afar, leaning against his locker as she holds Jordan's hand, observing them talking intimately outside the World Happiness Dance (where Angela's gaze imbues her with power, Brian's does the opposite — again, this is a girl's world). While he sometimes negotiates his way into Angela's circle (in the "Halloween" episode, for instance, or when his smarts are needed for tutoring or dismantling a bed), he doesn't quite fit. Brian occupies the outsider position Angela used to when she watched Rickie and Rayanne running off the school grounds and stared at Jordan Catalano as he dropped Visine in his eyes. And like Angela with Jordan, Brian considers her out of his "price range" (Angela on being alone with the more popular Jordan: "He's Jordan Catalano, he's not going to do anything!"), thinks about her "constantly" (Angela on Jordan: "I have nothing else on my mind"), and continues "being her little puppet" despite vowing not to. "I truly sicken myself," he says (Angela on the invite Jordan sends her after snubbing her: "The nauseating part is that I went"). And when Angela becomes the insider, steadfast Brian stays in the same spot.

Because Angela considers Jordan and Brian so antithetical, she can't even conceive of them populating the same space. "Jordan Catalano? At Brian Krakow's house?" she says in "Dancing in the Dark." "It's, like, against nature or something." She's narrowly typecast them (Brian has too, as evidenced by his inability to conceive of acquiring a girl's number even if it is through Jordan: "I don't believe this. You, like, do this? This is like how you live?") And, experiencing the world from her perspective, we do too. But we would have done it even without her help. "Bad boy" teens like *Rebel Without a Cause*'s Jim Stark, *The Breakfast Club*'s John Bender, and *Beverly Hills, 90210*'s Dylan McKay were Jordan's predecessors — it would be a few years before Brian types like Xander in *Buffy the Vampire Slayer* or Dawson in *Dawson's Creek* or Noel in *Felicity* would become viable romantic options. In 1994, Brians just didn't get the girl. So, four years later, when Devon Gummersall played a rapist in *Felicity*, we flipped. "It's like, what is Brian Krakow doing?" the actor said, speaking our minds in an interview with *Vulture*. Even after that, in 2014, we were surprised to see Brian turn up on the red carpet as a handsome 35-year-old. "Brian Krakow From *My So-Called Life* Is Hot Now," read the BuzzFeed headline that started the Brianaissance. "Angela Chase would totally go for THAT chiseled jawline now," Jessica Misener wrote, slipping between Brian and Gummersall as though they were one and the same. But Gummersall got it (Brian's no dummy, remember). "When you're a part of something like [*My So-Called Life*], it really just resonates so deeply with people, they are always going to see you as that character," he told *Vanity Fair*. So when he showed up in an episode of *Mad Men* in April 2015, the same thing happened. Elisabeth Moss, who played Peggy Olsen, found out Brian Krakow would be playing her love interest and "fucking flipped out." She had always been Team Brian.

It's Angela who brings Team Brian and Team Jordan together, figuratively (they are both in love with her) and literally (she signs up Jordan to be tutored by Brian). But she had some help. By the time she came along, the concept of "masculine gender role stress" had already been introduced. Two psychologists, Richard M. Eisler and Jay R. Skidmore, had discovered that certain masculine ideals — fitness, lack of emotion, and sexual and financial prowess — often caused emotional stress in men. In short, Western society has traditionally prized cold, powerful men who have lots of money and lots of sex. With the arrival of the women's liberation movement during the second wave, however, the definition of men's role in society started to shake loose as well. Male activists, alongside their feminist counterparts, began to question the male-as-breadwinner archetype and argued that masculinity and femininity were social constructs. The movement spawned the notion that men, just like Jordan Catalano and Brian Krakow, exist outside the binary they have been assigned. As Winnie Holzman told *Vulture*, "Even though Brian is tutoring Jordan, Jordan knows so much that Brian wants to know." And vice versa. Only by breaking out of the molds they have been born into can each of them, in the words of Graham Chase, who threw spaghetti at the wall of the masculine ideal way before them, "figure out how to be a man."

# 6

## Sex or a Conversation

*Rayanne:*
*You wanna have sex with him.*

*Angela:*
*Who?*

*Rayanne:*
*Who. Jordan. Catalano. Come on,*
*I'm not gonna tell anyone, just admit it.*

*Angela:*
*I just like how he's always leaning. Against stuff. He leans*
*great. Well, either sex or a conversation. Ideally both.*

Before Jordan Catalano, Angela Chase had only been kissed three times. Twice, really. The third time was the kiss of life, which is not technically a kiss. She's had the sex talk, of course — she's 15 — but she's never had sex. Chas(t)e Face can't even say it (she prefers the euphemism "um"). She can hardly think about it. Angela grew up in the AIDS generation — her doctor's sex talk? "I urge you to use a condom and a sponge" — so sex, to her, to many of us, is tantamount to disease. "I couldn't stop thinking about it," she says. "The, like, fact that people had sex. That they just had it, that sex was this thing people had, like a rash. Or a Rottweiler." Or an autoimmune disease.

The closest Angela gets to sex is an empty house that looks like a crack den ("People have been going there, you know, to have a place to go," Jordan says in "Pressure"). And, again, she likens copulation to a malady. "It was exactly like when I was waiting to get my flu shot only I didn't even get a magazine to read," she says. She doesn't go through with it. She tries to explain why in a language Jordan understands. "It's sort of like when you were letting me drive your car," she says. "And I loved it, it made me feel really powerful, but also really terrified, like I wasn't ready for that much freedom." Angela wants agency, just not sexual agency, "because sex made your whole life start, and if you think about life as like a circle or something, then sex and death are the same." There it is: sex is death, the ultimate loss. Angela will not claim her sexual agency because she can't stand losing her innocence. "The character most idealized on the show is a beautiful, able, middle class, white secular Christian virgin," writes Michele

Byers in *Dear Angela*. Angela's purity is the one thing that divides her from girls like Sharon and Rayanne, the one power she has over Jordan that they don't. Because it's Jordan who wistfully compares her to *Our Town*'s vanilla heroine with the words "she's always sayin' innocent stuff like that." How to lose that without losing what fundamentally defines her in the eyes of the world (or her world anyway)?

"[*MSCL*] presents the viewer with essentializing versions of adolescent female heterosexuality," Byers argues: "the innocent, the slut, the conformist." But as Holzman promised, the show introduces these stereotypes and then "busts" out of them. The adolescents in question (or two of them, anyway) consequently take issue with this reductive characterization when Jordan refuses to go public with his relationship with Angela. As Sharon says, "What, you're not cool enough for him to, like, be seen with you?" To which Rayanne replies, "Right, and she's not slutty enough for him to just do it with her and brag to his buds." The male characters have tropes of their own to tackle, but, when it comes to sex, they are off the hook. According to *Manifesta*, this is one of the many hypocrisies facing third wavers. "Not enough people are owning up to their sexual responsibilities," Jennifer Baumgardner and Amy Richards write, "and those who are tend to be female."

Sharon Cherski, the character most analogous to Angela in terms of provenance, may have had sex on her own terms — "I made a solemn promise to myself that I would not go all the way until I was ready," she says in "Why Jordan Can't Read," "and I'm, like, sticking to that" — but that choice temporarily gives her less agency, not more. As she explains to Angela, "after that, having sex was, like, expected, because, like, you can't go back. I mean, it kind of stopped mattering if I wanted to." The power briefly resides with her boyfriend, Kyle, which is highlighted in her incendiary teen-love poem in the *Liberty Lit*. "Haiku for Him" presents her lover as the more active member (so to speak) of the couple:

*He peels off my clothes like a starving man*
*Would peel an orange.*
*His lips taste my juicy sweetness.*
*My legs tangle with his;*
*We become one being,*
*A burning furnace*
*In the cold dark basement of love.*

That Liberty High's principal takes the magazine hostage — he says it's "unacceptable" because it does not meet "standards of decency" — is comparable to society taking teen girls' sexuality hostage. "This journal should be about giving students a voice, not about having their thoughts edited," says Vic Racine, the substitute who assigned Sharon's English class the writing exercise. "If these kids aren't afraid to put their hearts on the page, why should we be afraid of them?" But it's female hearts they fear the most, a shred of antediluvian residue that *MSCL* reveals we can't seem to wash off.

In her *Listen Up* essay "Lusting for Freedom," third-wave pioneer Rebecca Walker writes that sex "marks" girls. Angela

Chase concurs. "There's this dividing line between girls who have had sex, and girls who haven't," she says in "Pressure," threading this theme of sexual separation through her subsequent make-out sessions with Jordan Catalano. "My whole life became, like, divided into kissing and not kissing," she says. But kissing eventually overtakes everything. She starts to miss classes and lose marks. She feels guilty. Angela hasn't had sex yet, and she is already experiencing the fallout. The only way to avoid complete annihilation is to stop the process. In Byers' words, "The girl who is eminently desirable because she is forever innocent and is always fulfilling her role by saying no never loses."

Ipso facto, the biggest loser is the one who always says yes. Sharon's boyfriend dubs Rayanne "disgusting," for instance, for having sex with a guard at a museum in "Why Jordan Can't Read." In response, Sharon points out the double standard: "Face it, if a guy did that on a field trip, you and your friends would give him a medal." Yet she is not strong enough to say "yes" herself, not publicly anyway. Instead, she is happy to let everyone believe Rayanne wrote "Haiku for Him." As Bill Kte'pi explains in the *Dear Angela* essay "One of Those Fights Where It Feels Like the Fight's Having You," the differences between Sharon and Rayanne "are not so much about private behavior as public personae." Ostensibly, Sharon is a goody two-shoes who never makes a misstep. "I resolve to never again have sex with Kyle, or anyone, again unless I really love and respect them," she says in "Resolutions." Sex without love is, to her, a major misstep. So when she does it with Kyle, a guy she neither respects nor loves, she feels ashamed, even though so many boys before her have treated girls the same way with society's blessing. Gender norms demand that Sharon crave a relationship, not sex. As Walker explains, "Sex in silence and filled with shame is sex where our agency is denied. We need to learn that bodily pleasure belongs to us; it is our birthright."

Rayanne knows this. As she tells Sharon in "Resolutions," "you don't have to, like, be in love to have a good time." She is so sexually progressive that being slut-shamed (before that term was common parlance) doesn't faze her. "I have a right to live my own life," she says. Except that Rayanne is not having sex just to have a good time. She's having sex to fill a void. With no emotional fulfillment at home, she has to find it elsewhere. But nothing works, not even sex. "It's fun and all, you know. I don't always feel anything," she tells Sharon. "Sometimes I feel, like, numb or something."

Regardless of whether these characters' sex lives are being essentialized, that they are talking about them at all was progress in the narrow confines of network TV. In 1995, L. Monique Ward studied sexual themes in the shows most popular with teens — *Beverly Hills, 90210*; *Blossom*; *The Fresh Prince of Bel-Air*; etc. — and published her findings in the *Journal of Youth and Adolescence*. While she discovered that more than one in four interactions were sexual, it was the male characters who got all the action: "the sexual messages that occurred most frequently emphasized that sexual relations are a competition, that males see females as sexual objects and value women by their physical appearance, and that masculinity is linked with being sexual." Ward concluded, "Thus, the notions of males as sexual competitors and females as sexual objects were repeatedly emphasized." This chauvinistic approach had persisted despite the fact that the incidence of sexuality on TV had multiplied. In the pilot, for instance, Angela describes an incident in which Rayanne was almost assaulted:

*Angela:*
*These guys started hitting on us.*

*Brian:*
*What? Like, sexual harassment?*

*Angela:*
*Like, guys.*

By equating the word "guys" with "sexual harassment," Angela implies the two are interchangeable, that it's enough just to say "guys," because it is understood that guys are sexually aggressive toward women. Saying this to Brian suggests she is excluding him from her (erroneous) perception of "guys" in general. Rayanne seems to enforce the association after a false note circulates about Angela having sex with Jordan in his car; Rayanne thinks Jordan spread the rumor. "It's a very guy thing to do," she says. But it's a specific-guy thing to do. Note that Rayanne suggests it was Jordan who was responsible and not Brian, who also happened to be in the vicinity (Angela was in the car with Jordan, but the car was parked outside Brian's house), and who turns out to be the one who actually did it. But sexual bad behavior is considered the realm of alpha males, the most powerful men, like Jordan, not beta-brand Brians.

In 1996, the Kaiser Family Foundation, a U.S. nonprofit organization that focuses on national health, released a study of sexual content during family hour (8 to 9 p.m.). It revealed that even though sexual interactions had increased by 118 percent since 1986, only 12 percent involved teens, and the majority were limited to flirting and kissing (with rare mention of risk or responsibility). Of the shows that did mention being sexually responsible, almost a third already emphasized responsibility in the series as a whole. Canada's *Degrassi High*, for instance, which aired from 1989 to 1991, was one of the first shows to promote safe sex, having already covered teen pregnancy, abortion, gay rights, and AIDS. But the CBC franchise always did err on the side of dogma, according to Michele Byers, who also wrote *Growing Up Degrassi: Television, Identity and Youth Cultures*. "Teen shows are didactic; they're often meant to be instructive," she told me for a story in the *Toronto Star* in 2013. "There's been that criticism of *Degrassi* — that you were in health class every time it came on." *Beverly Hills, 90210* picked up the mantle and dressed it up, including an AIDS speaker, Kelly's rape confession at a slumber party, and Brenda's pregnancy scare in its first two seasons.

Though Ward found that female characters were not as sexually passive as previously perceived, the quality of sexual conversations on TV was undoubtedly gendered. Brenda Walsh made this observation way back in 1991 in the first season of *90210*, when her father questioned her choice to date Dylan: "Why is it with Brandon you just wanted to make sure he knew about birth control but my whole value system is on the line?" Her dad's response? "Brenda, it's different with girls." It certainly is for Angela, whose sexuality on *MSCL* is policed by her mom (in "Guns and Gossip" her mom straight-up says, "I don't think you're ready."). Sharon, meanwhile, recalls Allison in *The Breakfast Club* — "Well, if you say you haven't, you're a prude. If you say you have, you're a slut. It's a trap." — when she expresses fear over having sex with a guy she doesn't respect. "I can't become the type of person that would 'use' another person," she tells Rayanne in "Resolutions," "because I could end up like you!" Rayanne, however, is safe. The "family values" of this poor, promiscuous, substance-abusing waif from a broken home cannot be threatened because she has none to begin with. The men have it even easier. Where Rayanne is called a slut, no one comments on male analogue Jordan Catalano's lifestyle. If anything, his collection of sexual partners is evidence of his appeal (and, in keeping with Ward's study, his masculinity). And while Brian is considered as virginal as Angela, the fact that he gets an erection by touching a female classmate's hand or that, as Graham suggests, he spends much of his time picturing Angela naked, is more of a punchline than a problem. Rickie's sexuality, meanwhile, being neither clearly gendered nor clearly aligned, is barely discussed at all.

The boys have inherited their forefathers' approach to sex. To Jordan, as to Angela's dad, Graham (not to mention

Tony Poole, Patty's ex-boyfriend, with whom she "did some pretty crazy and wild things"), a kiss is never just a kiss. As Angela's mom chides her husband in "Dancing in the Dark," "A kiss must lead somewhere. Where do they drill that into you? Shop class?" As we know, Jordan never skips shop. After he and Angela eventually start making out, he evokes Graham when he says in "Pressure," "How long are we supposed to keep doing this?" Later Jordan uses the same words — "supposed to" — when he pressures Angela to have sex. "It's accepted," he says, somewhat desperately. "Unless you're, like, abnormal." The word "normal" is used a few times with respect to Angela's love life. "I've never had an actual boyfriend," she says. "I don't know if that's normal or not." And during an appointment with her doctor, she asks "what's normal" when it comes to sex.

"Normal" for Jordan would be for him to have all the power and for Angela to have none. But this privilege is "relative and contextual," as Roxane Gay wrote in *Bad Feminist*. ("To have privilege in one or more areas does not mean you are wholly privileged.") Jordan's power is determined by three things (two of them variable): his gender, his location, and being the object of affection. By virtue of being a man, he benefits from male sexual privilege, which means he gets to be promiscuous without consequence, to have sex without loss. Early on in *MSCL*, a note is passed around Liberty High which states, "angela & jordan catalano complete sex!! in his car . . . can you believe her??" Not only is Angela not afforded a full name, she is the one criticized for their rumored encounter. Jordan is free of sexual responsibility; she is not. As for location, high school is the space where Jordan claims power, which he cannot assert in his home life. At Liberty he has social prowess, it is his turf, and Angela, not even enough of an entity to make the top 40 list, endangers that. By lowering his social status, she threatens to render him as powerless at school as he is at home, so, yes, he will date her, but only if he calls the shots. So he controls their rendezvous, which invariably fall into his comfort zones: his car, the boiler room, an abandoned house. "Angela, you're letting Jordan Catalano, like, control you," Rayanne says in "Self-Esteem." And by engaging in a sexual relationship with Jordan in "Betrayal," Rayanne gleans some of this power from him. "You can't let their stupid actions control you," Rickie cautions Angela. But she can't help it.

Angela's obsession with Jordan is so potent that it obscures everything else. "What's amazing is when you can feel your life going somewhere," she says in "Dancing in the Dark" when she finds herself alone in Jordan's car with him for the first time. "Like, your life just figured out how to get good. Like, that second." Jordan's behavior determines hers. When he doesn't show up for their date, she dresses in mourning. When he does, she is elated. In "On the Wagon," she even fantasizes about him controlling her: "You must have me as your own. You can't live another second knowing others could possess me." But she bestows that power on him. Because the consequence of being the object of affection is that you are given power over the subject — Jordan is in a privileged position because Angela's crush gives him that privilege. This privilege is not, however, systemic, just as hers is not. In certain contexts, she is privileged and Jordan is not; in others, he is and she isn't. For instance, in "Pressure," Jordan shows up at Angela's door in the middle of the night, which is his means (intentional or otherwise) of disorienting Angela in her own space. Then, in the liminal space of his own open garage, he loses control, futilely raising his voice at Angela after she refuses to sleep with him: "It's what you're supposed to do!" In response, she walks away. And when she breaks up with him — *she* breaks up with *him* — in her own home, she is positioned on the top step of her staircase; once again, she is the one with the power.

The Jordan Angela wants to possess is not the Jordan who exists in the world. In the second episode, she hesitates to meet him for the first time because "if you make it real, it's not the same. It's not yours anymore. I don't know, maybe I'd rather have the fantasy than even him." The fantasy is all potential; the reality is inevitable disappointment. On Halloween, Angela drifts back in time to fraternize with '60s "greaser" Nicky Driscoll, whom she mistakenly-not-mistakenly calls Nicky Catalano and who has a habit of transforming into Jordan in the school staircase. Angela wanders around Liberty High searching for Nicky, only to find his girlfriend confessing, "Nicky Driscoll is going nowhere, and I'm not going there with him." Is Angela as shallow as this bobby-socked teen? As her mother says, "It's always tempting to lose yourself with someone who's maybe lost themselves, but, eventually, you want reality." Angela's reality is so tied to control that its pull crosses generations from her mother to her — the foray into rebellion is inevitably drawn back to the familiar, the safe. So when Angela hears that Rayanne and Jordan slept together in "Betrayal," she no longer wants to go anywhere with any of these people, all of whom represent a break from her stable domicile. "I have to be alone," she tells Rickie. "I mean, like, for years." Yet being home alone is not the same anymore. Her innocence, that thing that once made her so desirable, now implies, as Anastasia Higginbotham writes in *Listen Up*, "immaturity, stupidity, and a death of passion."

As regressive as it is to equate virginity with innocence, it is impossible to deny society's loaded perception of adolescent female sexuality. Angela acknowledges that; of boys, she says in "Pressure," "they only care about — you know, getting you into bed, or something." By resisting Jordan, a boy who emotionally consumes her to such an extent that he effectively controls her, Angela is able to retain some level of authority. In a moment of foreshadowing in the pilot, she finds herself alone for the first time with Jordan while the Divinyls' "I Touch Myself" music video plays soundlessly in the foreground. The 1990 lead single from the Aussie band's album *diVINYLS* was controversial at the time for promoting female masturbation. That it is playing while Angela sits alone with Jordan signals not only the sexual tension she feels, but also her ability to sate herself on her own terms. Along those lines, one of Angela's most ecstatic moments in the series (in "Betrayal") takes place when she is alone in bed.

We open on Angela's face, her head on her pillow, her expression serious, as her voice-over professes: "I loved Jordan

Catalano so much, and talked about him so much and thought about him so much, it was like he lived inside me. Like he had taken possession of my soul, or something . . . and then one day . . ." — and then those drum beats, like exclamation points, four of them, pulling her lips into a smile so wide, her cheek dimples — ". . . I got over him!" Suddenly Angela is thrashing around her room to Violent Femmes' "Blister in the Sun," somersaulting and jumping and head-banging and singing. Long rumored to be a hymn to masturbation, songwriter Gordon Gano told the *Village Voice* in 2013 that was not his intention. The 1983 earworm from Violent Femmes' self-titled debut was more likely about drug addiction. And that interpretation works just as well for *MSCL* since Angela is basically hooked on Jordan — "It was like he had been surgically removed from my heart and I was free."

Except she isn't, because they've broken up over the wrong thing. Their connection is based not on copulation (or not entirely), but on something far more complex. Rebecca Walker advised third wavers to liberate sex "from pussy and dick and fucking" and from the institution of family. "It can be more: more sensual, more spiritual, more about communication and healing," she wrote. "If sex is about communicating, let us think about what we want to say and how will we say it." Angela already has: sex and a conversation. And, already, the first time Jordan kisses her, in "Dancing in the Dark," he fails to live up to that when his lips interrupt her mid-conversation. "I was talking," she says, pushing him away. When it happens a second time, she is even less reserved. "Quit it!" she shouts.

"I mean, you have to work up to that." Jordan's response? "You talk a lot."

In short, Jordan precludes Angela's ability to communicate. When he's not kissing the girl who is obsessed with him, his very existence is otherwise muffling her. "If Jordan Catalano is, like, nearby, my entire body knows it, like one of those dogs that point," Angela says. "I'll keep talking and stuff, but my mind won't even know what I'm saying." Unable to speak it, Angela writes it down. She commits "every feeling I've ever wanted to express about Jordan Catalano" to a letter to him. But the letter is not meant to be delivered. And when it is, in a blatantly symbolic move, Jordan is unable to read it. In other words, there is a fundamental inability for Angela and Jordan to communicate. It's the one thing she wants to do and the one thing she can't. "I can't even communicate with him when it matters," she says in "Halloween" after Jordan pays little heed to her warning that he could be kicked out of class. "When it could affect his, like, life." Conversations go two ways, and Jordan is unable, or perhaps unwilling, to reciprocate.

"Red" perfectly captures this discord. After Angela discovers that Jordan has trouble reading in "Why Jordan Can't Read," he invites her to watch him rehearse with his band, Frozen Embryos (a fitting name for a guy who has difficulty developing or changing). He then performs an acoustic version of the tune she heard him humming earlier in the day ("Is that a Crowded House song?") about a "her" called Red, whom he considers his safe haven. ("I've wished in retrospect that I made the lyrics a little different," Holzman says. "I think

I could have gone much, much darker.") Angela takes it as a metaphor; Jordan doesn't know what a metaphor is. After serenading her, he promises to meet her parents but never turns up. As Angela waits, Jordan's voice is heard humming his song, which has no doubt been in her head since she first heard it. He slowly sings the last two verses to drive it home, so to speak. Because "Red" is not actually about her, but his car, the symbol of his masculinity, his home without a home, a masculinity that Angela threatens to subvert. "It's like she knows too much about me, or something," he tells Rickie as an excuse for not showing up to the Chases. "She just makes too big a deal about everything. She makes everything too complicated." He's just trying to keep things simple, and so Angela is never told the song is not about her. Instead, she is surrounded by music that plays off her inability to connect with the guy she loves: "Dreams" by The Cranberries, "Try" by Billy Pilgrim, The Lemonheads' "Dawn Can't Decide."

When Jordan discloses his illiteracy — "I never told anyone before" — Angela considers it an ersatz valentine. Not only is this their first shared secret, suggesting a newfound intimacy, it also presents hope. There is now a reason for their disconnect, so it is conceivable that they might overcome it. "I understand him in this way I didn't even know existed," Angela tells Rayanne. "And it has completely changed everything. Everything." But, in the end, it hasn't. In the last episode of the series, Angela dreams she is chasing Jordan. "The end of the dream is always the same. I catch up with him. I yell and scream how he hurt and betrayed me. How I can never forgive him," she says in voice-over. "He just stands there, like someone caught in a storm who stopped caring how wet he gets."[9] The image is reminiscent of the closing scene in Christine Doza's *Listen Up* essay "Bloodlove," in which she screams and screams, "and we make a wailing wall, all of us screaming at the tops of our lungs, screaming for our lives, and no one is listening, nothing is changing."

The only way for Jordan to be the person Angela wants him to be is to know Angela, and the only one who really knows Angela is Brian Krakow. But when Sharon Cherski tells her in "Strangers in the House" that Brian is "obviously in love with you," Angela laughs in mortification. "Brian Krakow is not in love with me!" she guffaws. Angela is so convinced of this that she later, heartbreakingly, confronts Brian with the following missive on love: "I cannot wait until it happens to you because I'm gonna look at you, and I'm gonna laugh, and I'll say, 'See? See? I told you so.'" On *The Complete Series*, Winnie Holzman explained that a relationship between Angela and Brian would be "too confronting" while Jordan is "the fantasy."

Angela wants both the reality and the fantasy. After betraying her, Jordan attempts to apologize, but he can't. He is unable to get through to her with his own words, and it's only when he uses Brian's voice in "In Dreams Begin Responsibilities" that fantasy and reality fuse. "I did an undefendable thing. I created

---

9 The final episode of the series is named after poet Delmore Schwartz's 1937 short story, "In Dreams Begin Responsibilities," in which the narrator dreams he is in a movie theater watching his parents and tries to influence the outcome of their crumbling relationship by yelling at the screen. "It wasn't so much what that story was about or that I was emulating that story, per se," Winnie Holzman tells me. "It was much more that I loved that exact phrase."

my own prison and I have to exist in it," he says. "Maybe I had a wish, or whatever, to punish you. An unconscious wish." So pleased is Angela with her fantasy becoming a reality that she doesn't even bother to ask how it happened. "It was like a dream, you would not believe the brilliantly insightful words that came out of his mouth," she tells Rickie. "Then, just as I'm realizing there's hope that we could actually communicate, he runs away." It's like a fairy tale (reminiscent of Angela's description of her mother's ancient adolescent relationship with Tony Poole — not to mention the fable she wrote — "Long, long ago," she says. "Like a fairy tale"), and Angela gets swept up in the pumpkinness of it all. "She's, like, starved, or something," Jordan says. "It's gotta be written down so I can't screw up." And with that, he seals his fate. That Brian writes the letter that Angela falls for is proof that he can connect with her in a way that Jordan cannot (Brian again betrays his similarity to Angela by using the same method she used with Jordan to communicate to her what he can't in person). It's Brian whose voice reads it out, because it's Brian who wrote it. It's he who, in essence, first makes love to Angela.

> *Dear Angela, I know in the past I've caused you pain and I'm sorry. And I'll always be sorry till the day I die. And I hate this pen I'm holding because I should be holding you. I hate this paper under my hand because it isn't you. I even hate this letter because it's not the whole truth. Because the whole truth is so much more than a letter can even say. If you want to hate me, go ahead. If you want to burn this*

*letter, do it. You could burn the whole world down; you could*
*tell me to go to hell. I'd go, if you wanted me to. And I'd*
*send you a letter from there. Sincerely, Jordan Catalano*

Winnie Holzman adapted the letter's content from Edmond
Rostand's 19th-century play *Cyrano de Bergerac*. "I wanted to
show Brian's desperation, his intensity, and also the uncondi-
tional aspect of his love," she told *Vulture*. Using Jordan just as
much as Jordan was using him, Brian was "speaking right from
his soul," and what is love to Angela if not that? As she says,
"Love is when you look into someone's eyes, and suddenly,
you go all the way inside to their soul, and you both know,
instantly." Or maybe just she does; as the letter states, she is
the one who takes precedence, not the truth. "I didn't like it, I
loved it," she tells Jordan. "I loved it." And, for the first time,
she's the one who kisses him. By uniting fantasy and reality, by
finally connecting with Jordan — regardless of whether or not
he is behind it — Angela claims her sexual agency.

And by telling Angela how he feels, Brian does too. "I
think in a way Angela always knew it wasn't Jordan," Holzman
told *Vulture* in 2014, "because that wasn't the voice of Jordan
Catalano and that was not a move that Jordan Catalano could
really pull." In the same interview, she elaborated, "The fact
that Jordan couldn't write that letter doesn't mean he didn't
have things he wanted to say. He didn't feel like he could write
a letter. That wasn't his worldview of himself. He's dyslexic. He
had trouble reading. His image of himself, I think, could never
write a letter . . ." What matters is that he didn't. And in the last

episode of the series, Brian inadvertently admits that to Angela — "I meant every word," he slips — and everything changes (for real this time). Though Angela ends up in Jordan's car, it's Brian she is watching as they drive away; he's the one who commands her attention, not Jordan. "Forget what I said. Forget this whole conversation," Brian tells her. But, of course, she can't. Sex or a conversation, that was the deal. So Angela responds with a question — "How?" — her way of keeping the conversation open. In an interview with *Vulture* years later, Holzman outlined how she saw the Brian-Angela dialogue unfolding: "She would be in a relationship with Jordan, Brian would be in a relationship with Delia, and they would be longing for each other, basically." The two of them sentenced to a never-ending conversation neither of them will admit to having.

# 7

## Strangers in the House

The second-last scene of *My So-Called Life*'s pilot may not present the most iconic Patty Chase image, but it may be the most on point. In the glow of her Laura Ashley bedroom set, Angela's mother is alone, wearing a ruffled white night dress amid a ruffled pile of papers — she is crunching numbers for the business she has long since taken over from her father — while her husband stands outside with another woman. It's a portrait of a second waver caught between her recurring dreams about Princess Di and her recurring thoughts about Hillary Clinton. This is the woman who goes as Rapunzel in the "Halloween" episode because the First Lady costume is already taken. This is the woman who thinks "Princesses don't get divorced," but smashes her childhood Cinderella anyway. While she sits in her wholesome cotton, on the TV Shirley

Temple sits in hers. And in front of it stands Patty's daughter, Angela. "My mother's adopted," she says in voice-over. "So for a while, she was looking for her real parents. I guess that's just what everyone's looking for." Most of us couldn't find them on television. In 2003's *Television Families: Is Something Wrong in Suburbia?*, author William Douglas found that most families on the small screen were middle-class suburbanites. "Real suburbia favored white Americans over minorities, young over old, parenthood over childlessness, and affluence over poverty," he wrote, noting that the same went for TV. These clans were also mostly relegated to comedy since, before the so-called Golden Age of Television, drama didn't often rely on the "mundane realism" of domesticity for narrative motivation. In that sense, *MSCL*, which reportedly reached a demographic that was 85 percent non-teens, was revolutionary.

The complex authenticity that Winnie Holzman imbued in Angela and her friends extended to Patty and Graham and their peers. These adults were given more screen time when Claire Danes's juvenile hours limited hers; according to the *New Yorker*, Holzman decided to "change the nature of the show" in order to work around its lead's schedule. "In that moment, we decided to include the lives of the parents more," Herskovitz said. The show was never meant just for kids anyway; otherwise, it would have veered closer to the trend of its contemporaries, which put teens in primary roles and parents as support. *The Wonder Years* offered a rare example of fully formed adults, but *MSCL* went even further to make them as ambivalent as the adolescents, an acknowledgment of the fact that ambiguity is perennial. The adults' struggles mirror those of their children, it's just that they are exploring their identities as grown-ups. Rather than the battlefield of school, the domestic sphere, the work sphere, the parental sphere are where the adults wage their war. And while their children are central to their lives — despite the fact that mom and dad don't have all the answers, and don't have all the right ones even when they do — the children themselves are more concerned with their own lives than their parents'. Pushing one's parents away is often part of forging one's own identity — the first step in finding who you are is often finding who you aren't. Still, each character's roots are established at home, which is often defined by the materfamilias.

"Mom, you couldn't possibly understand or help," Angela says when Patty tries to in "Guns and Gossip." Angela believes this so strongly that when her parents do get her right, she is shocked. "It's so strange how parents can, out of nowhere, turn psychic," she says in the second episode. "It's unnerving." Angela alludes to their conflicting personalities in "The Zit" as she and Patty try on identical outfits for the mother-daughter fashion show, designating them a "warped version of *The Patty Duke Show*," the '60s sitcom about identical cousins with opposing personas. Angela's dad characterizes Patty more positively. "Everything she does is for you," Graham says in the pilot, to which Angela responds, "It's just obvious she's always looking for someone to blame." Both are true.

Second-wave feminism brought up Patty Chase. In the wake of the previous generation's suffragettes, women expanded equal rights from the voting booth to the workplace. Their rallying cry was Betty Friedan's *The Feminine Mystique*: "I want something more than my husband and my children and my home." The men's response? "I want something more than my job." Patty's something more is her family printing business. Like her daughter, she is on the cusp of change when we meet her and, like her daughter, she changes her hair to prove it — or, at least, actress Bess Armstrong did it for her. "I said to [Winnie Holzman], 'I'm sick of everybody assuming that I'm exactly the same person I was when I was 23,'" Armstrong told ForeverYoungAdult.com in 2013. "'I feel like I want to chop it off so that people will see me as more grown-up.'" Angela and her mother share multiple experiences like this ("Mom, just 'cause I changed my hair doesn't mean you should," she tells Patty in "Dancing in the Dark"), from Patty's own high-school beau being a Jordan Catalano type to her relationship with a Rayanne-like friend who OD'd, to the verbal tics ("in my humble opinion") and the contradictions ("I'm not even that upset," Patty says about a tardy Angela in the pilot, before exclaiming upon her daughter's arrival, "Where the hell have you been?"). Yet Angela is convinced they have nothing in common.

Patty is what *Manifesta* dubbed the "martyr mom," a passive aggressive who sacrifices herself for her family but would rather be doing anything else (in Patty's case, working). She is dependable and wholesome and does "what's right" ("I cannot bring myself to eat a well-balanced meal in front of my mother," Angela says in the pilot. "It just means too much to her.") with a Stepford smile etched on her face. But her daughter sees through the act. "Sometimes I think if my mother wasn't so good at pretending to be happy, she'd be better at actually being happy," Angela says in "Other People's Mothers." But Patty seems destined to exist between being and pretense because even though she is personally empowered, she hasn't extricated herself from the traditional role society has doled out for her — the one she embodied as a high-school prom queen — so she tries to appease both simultaneously. Angela's desire to stab her mom repeatedly in the pilot after Patty makes a quip about her daughter's new hair is actually a desire to stab repeatedly the system that turned Patty into this split personality. "The tension between the second and third waves of feminism is similar to the squeamishness and stress between mothers and daughters," write Baumgardner and Richards in *Manifesta*. "On a political level, girls who reject their mothers are usually rejecting the roles cast for them by a patriarchal society."

Patty was born into a generation that believed raising a girl meant "walking on eggshells half the time" and that father knows best. "He's never really known what I'm worth," Patty says of her own dad, who has less business acumen than the daughter he bequeathed his company to. Despite realizing that she's in the grip of a gender role prescribed to her by an inequitable culture, Patty is unable to extract herself. When her dance teacher says it's the man who "goes forward most frequently" in "Dancing in the Dark," Patty sasses, "Tell me about it." She is 40, possibly pre-menopause — "Is that like pre-death?" — and has gained seven pounds and lines that won't go away. "I, like all women, am becoming less and less attractive in the eyes of the world and more and more expendable as I grow older," she tells her husband in "The Zit," "while you, like all men, are considered more desirable and more attractive the older you get. Of course, you'll die sooner." Patty doesn't even seem to consider her body fully her own. After a pregnancy scare in "Why Jordan Can't Read," she confesses, "I feel such relief, such gratitude for my life, my freedom" (the refusal to even acknowledge abortion as an option signals a patriarchal hangover). When she considers cutting her hair short, her best friend, Camille Cherski, cautions her that men like long hair — and the color red. "Who cares what they like?" Patty responds. "But they supposedly like variety, right?" She ends up cutting it *and* wearing red, a compromise to match her compromised empowerment, the push and pull between past and progress.

This ambivalence extends to her relationship with her husband. "Couples who enact conventional gender roles," Douglas wrote in *Television Families*, "are seen as more satisfied than couples who divide familial rights and responsibilities in other ways." Patty and Graham are not conventional. On most shows, the dad does the problem-solving and discipline, while the mom is nurturing and domestic. On *MSCL*, it's the opposite. And while Graham is initially Angela's preferred parent — on trend with most family series — this changes quickly when she suspects that her dad might be an adulterer. As Patty says of her own father, whom she finally sees as fallible in "Father Figures," "I've turned some sort of corner with this, and I can't go back." Patty is relieved that Angela has turned this corner a lot sooner. "You have to let her push you away and not punish her for it," she tells Graham. "All she's doing is pushing you off your pedestal, and she's right to do it, she has to do it, she's right on schedule. She's not a thousand years late like I am."

The pedestal was erected by his daughters, not his wife. Struggling with familial scheduling in "The Substitute," Patty quips to her husband, "You know what we need? A wife." Up until that point, Graham has been good enough. He is the man Patty "partly" married because she knew he would be "a really good father." It's a gendered flip of the old cliché that men choose women who will make a good home for them. And it's one of many in the Patty-Graham dyad. According to Douglas, while contemporary TV narratives exhibit a balance of economic power between spouses — only between 4 and 14 percent of TV wives are homemakers — despite their relatively equal employment, the men's personalities are generally characterized as more active and dominant, the women's as passive and submissive. On *MSCL*, it's the opposite. Patty wears the pants both at home and at work; their high school dynamic — she was the prom queen, Graham couldn't get a date — has stretched into their marriage. "She's kind of my dad's boss now," Angela explains in the pilot, "which I guess he tries not to think about." In a world of equality, this would imply that, with Patty being allowed to break out of her mold, Graham would be permitted to do the same. During the second wave, men's liberation groups were established for this very purpose — to expand the male role in society beyond that of the strong, silent provider. It wasn't particularly successful. Men like Graham are still expected to embody the convention of primary breadwinner even when their wives have already cast themselves in the role. Graham, despite the amount of work he puts in at home and at his wife's business, is considered by his very orthodox father-in-law to be "sponging off" Patty because she brings home the bacon — who cooks it is beside the point. Patty picks up where her dad leaves off, calling Graham "defeatist" for his lack of confidence at work, which implies she is also calling him out for his inability to be an assertive alpha male. But neither does she expect him to excel at home. She is shocked at Graham's decorating abilities — "I guess we found another thing you can do," she exclaims of his wallpapering in "The Life of Brian" — and of his talents in the kitchen, she patronizes, "Graham is emotional about food." It is only when he turns his hobby into an actual career — cooking class teacher, then head chef at a restaurant — that she supports him. Graham takes on the domestic role traditionally adopted by women, sewing on a merit badge for Danielle (which no doubt boasts better stitching than Patty's infamous mother-daughter pageant frocks) and peacekeeping in the home. But where women are praised for nurturing, he is characterized by Angela's substitute, Vic, as "fragile." As for his wife's independence, Graham adopts the familiar stance of the woman who stands by her man, preferring to prop up his powerful wife. "I like it when you actually need me," he tells Patty, which recalls Camille's comment to Patty about her ailing husband, Andy, "I need him; I'm not like you."

But it's hard to need someone who isn't sure who they are. Like Angela and Patty, Graham too is searching for his identity.

In another break from tradition, instead of being the stable adult male — the sun around which his family orbits — he is as in flux as his teenage daughter and her male peers ("Life of Brian" has Graham, Brian, and Jordan all connected by the mantra "whatever happens, happens"). His quest is for meaningful work; with that, both he and Patty hope their marriage will improve. In "Strangers in the House," after hearing that Andy Cherski, who has just had a heart attack, lives for his job, Graham says, "It must be great to feel that way." Soon after, Patty fires him — "Working together is pushing us apart," she says — becoming his agent of change (she is the stronger one after all). "What'll I do," Graham laments, to which Patty responds, "I guess you're finally going to figure it out." But she again is the one who forces him do that by enrolling him in a cooking class, where he eventually finds his niche. "It's not that I like to cook," he explains. "It's this thing I can just do. The one thing I can do." Graham moves from his domestic role to another traditionally feminine role outside the home, maintaining his status as submissive in the Patty-Graham dynamic. Little wonder he gravitates toward Hallie Lowenthal, a strong woman not unlike his wife, but one who needs him — to explain cooking to her, to cook for her restaurant — and considers his talent a strength rather than a curiosity.

Angela feels as let down by her father as Patty eventually does by hers. "My dad and I used to be pretty tight," she says in the first episode. "The sad truth is my breasts have come between us." She appears to resent Graham for playing into society's regressive belief that there is a fundamental separation between men and women. "She acts so distant, with a sort of silent contempt," Graham notes in "Father Figures." But if she's contemptuous, it's because her father has betrayed her twofold: by aligning himself with the patriarchy and by potentially cheating on her mother (not to mention, in her eyes as in her mother's, his inability, or perhaps his unwillingness, to stand up to Patty while his own daughter attempts to stand up to everyone). The latter leads Angela to conflate Jordan and her father in a dream that comes in the wake of Jordan's betrayal. "Dad not wanting to look at me is, like, the worst feeling," she says in "Father Figures," which is later reflected by Jordan ignoring her in her dream in "In Dreams Come Responsibilities." Graham is acting aloof after trying to reconnect with Angela by giving her two Grateful Dead tickets. But, ever her mother's daughter, Angela wants to be the one to control her relationship, wants to be the one with the power. She implies her father forfeited that power when she first suspected him of cheating, but really he forfeited it when he started treating her differently post-puberty and she, simultaneously, started having mixed feelings about him. "When you're not sure you trust a person anymore — say, a person you really trusted; say your father — you start wishing they'd do something, like, really wrong, just so you could be right about them," she says.

So Angela jealously watches as her dad kisses her prepubescent sister, Danielle, and teaches Rayanne how to cook,[10] but rejects his attention just the same. Selling the Grateful Dead

---

10 "When someone compliments your parents, there's like nothing to say," Angela (ironically) says. "It's like a stun gun to your brain."

tickets he gives her as a gift in "Father Figures" is her attempt at reclaiming some of the control she has lost. "I saw the Grateful Dead when I was 15 years old," Graham tells Patty. "It was one of the eight best nights of my life. It's something I wanted to give her." By rejecting this, Angela is rejecting Graham's very essence, though perhaps, more largely, she is rejecting his generation, the same way she rejects her mother's.

Though she could be construed as simple comic relief, Angela's younger sister, Danielle, like her parents, offers a break from Angela's perspective, keeping us from wholly siding with her and preserving the show's ambiguous narrative. That Danielle gets along with their father is one of the many disparities between the two of them. The first words out of her mouth are "I would never dye my hair red." That her first sentence is defined by her older sister (and, more specifically, contradicts her) is emblematic of her entire character. Danielle is constantly eclipsed by her older sibling and, as a result, is constantly trying to get noticed. "What do you do, keep, like, a running tally of everything we buy for Angela?" Danielle's dad asks on Christmas. "Yes," she replies. It's the only way for her to be acknowledged. But, still, she isn't. Danielle literally stands on her head to get attention, only to be ignored again and again and again by her family and by Brian and by the world. (Even the directors often push her out of the center of the frame, so the audience no longer pays attention to her either.)

Like Angela, Danielle exercises control in her life by claiming agency within the confines of it, presenting herself as her sister's opposite. Where Angela is serious, she is humorous. Where Angela shuns the fashion show, she welcomes it. Where Angela rejects Brian Krakow, she flirts with him. Yet nothing Danielle says can ever measure up to what Angela says: bisexuality vs. gym class, a dance club vs. a horror movie, a school shooting vs. a kid tripping, a school walkout vs. thin mints. "It's truly amazing," the 10-year-old says in her voice-over episode, "Weekend." "I have the power to be invisible." Unsurprisingly, one of the rare times that Danielle commands her parents' attention for an extended period of time is in the Halloween episode when she dresses up (and acts) like Angela — short red wig, her sister's plaid shirt, Doc Martens — which is, essentially, her reason for doing it. Angela's the center of attention, not Danielle, ergo Danielle becomes Angela. "I hate her," Danielle tells Sharon of her sister. "I do." To which Sharon replies, "So why'd you want to be her if you hate her so much?" The morning after, we see Danielle reverentially put her sister's folded clothes back, touching her shirt wistfully. "Bet you're glad to be yourself again, huh?" her mom says. Though Danielle nods, her mirthless smile betrays how she really feels about retreating back into the role of forgotten younger sibling.

Danielle's invisibility is tied to her innocence, which is highlighted by the fact that she is almost always situated within the realm of the Chase home. She is safe as houses, unlike her sister. Angela commands so much attention because her life is no longer tethered to her parents' — it's unpredictable. Danielle can pretend to be as outlandish as she wants, but she is protected because of her youth, even within her own home. "My life is different people kicking me out of different rooms," she says. But, again, she exerts power where she can. After complaining about her life being "edited," she refuses to be edited herself. "Am I allowed to have a feeling in this house or is that just Angela?" she asks. And *MSCL* responds by giving her voice its own episode, making her the only other character besides Angela and Brian who is granted an interior monologue. Fittingly, it is in an episode in which Rayanne is handcuffed to the Chases' bed (they are out of town). While designated parent Angela, as well as Brian, Sharon, and Rickie are all present to help free Rayanne, it is the latter with whom Danielle seems to find the most affinity (inevitable when you consider how connected Rayanne is to Angela). "My whole life is waiting for something to happen," Danielle says at the beginning of the episode, which is later echoed by Rayanne in a private moment between the two of them. It's one of the many instances in which Danielle's invisibility allows her to be privy to information others are not (like Rickie, who also has the "power to be invisible," not because of his age but because of his race, class, and sexuality). Often this takes the form of information about Angela's love life, but, still, it's an example of the young being more in sync with each other than they are with adults. It's Angela after all who hears Danielle begging to be in the mother-daughter fashion show when her mom does not. As much as she may be vexed by her little sister, she understands her — Danielle is what Angela used to be; she is a constant reminder of who Angela once was. Which is why they so often don't get along — Angela's rejection of Danielle is a rejection of her past. That they are bonded by blood, however, underscores the complexity of the Chases' relationships. Despite their attempts to forge their individuality, they are united under a shared roof. *MSCL* reminds us that even in the most familiar spaces, even within the comforts of home, uncertainty dwells.

# 8

## Go, Now, Go

*My So-Called Life* lived and died before getting anywhere near its own adolescence. On May 16, 1995, less than four months after the last episode aired, ABC officially canceled it. "Unfortunately, *My So-Called Life*'s performance last season and all indications for the future suggest that its appeal is far too narrow," the network's statement read. The show reportedly had an audience of 10 million (for comparison, hitcom *Home Improvement* had three times that number), the "core" of which was teen girls. Co-creator Marshall Herskovitz told the *Hartford Courant* that a teen girl also killed it. "My understanding is that [Claire Danes's] agent called the network three weeks ago and told them that she didn't want to come back," he said. The actress's publicist denied this, but Herskovitz insisted she was gravitating toward the big screen. "I think she wants to make movies because she feels the environment is more conducive to what she wants to do," he said. "She made known her preference for that."

So the fans blamed Danes, and she ignored them. "I can't assume responsibility," she told *Vulture* 16 years later. "A 14-year-old is not going to determine the fate of a network show." And, essentially, she is right; ABC could have held her to her contract. But Danes was also the reason the show was what it was. It couldn't have existed without her any more than it could have existed without its creator, Winnie Holzman. If Danes left, there was no show, but, in the execs' eyes, if she stayed, there wasn't much of one either. "Networks didn't understand that you could sell to adolescent girls," Herskovitz said on *The Complete Series*. "They didn't care about them. They were sort of an invisible demographic."

*MSCL* made them visible. The show spoke to and for them, capturing their search for identity, the disconnect they felt from their mothers and fathers, and their struggles with gender, class, race, and sexuality. So their campaign to save *MSCL* wasn't merely a fight to save the show; it was a fight to save themselves. As Susan Murray wrote in *Dear Angela*, "the importance of Angela (who teens have adopted as an ideal or perhaps symbolic self) is that she has become, at least to this small group, a contested site where they can enact a tiny battle of visibility." And they chose the Internet as their battleground. By 1993, the public had access to the internet through AOL, which had previously been relegated to the world of academia. *MSCL* fans, nicknamed "Lifers," took over ABC's nascent bulletin board, inundating it with thousands of posts. The entries revolved largely around these teens' searches for their identities, a theme that paralleled that of the show. "Just as *MSCL* supplies a narrative atmosphere through which self-reflection is induced," wrote Murray, "the online board provides the opportunity for further engagement with both the show and the self." Lifers would chat about *MSCL* and post their own fan fiction, forming relationships with like-minded individuals that further strengthened their fandom.

The online interests of these alternative teens were already being bolstered by print media. The late '80s and early '90s bloomed with more realistic magazines aimed at young women — *Sassy*, *Bust*, *Bitch* — forming a community for girls that didn't shill idealistic expectations. Instead, these publications reflected their multi-faceted lives back to them, in much the same way as *MSCL*. *Sassy* even featured a zine of the month, which, according to *Manifesta*, legitimized "the DIY publications at a time when zines were the only place where people who were too young, punk, or weird, such as riot grrrls, could publish." *Sassy* also refused to pander to big-name celebrities or hold them up as the sole icons for young women, instead pushing unconventional girls like Chloë Sevigny and Claire Danes (*Sassy* was, in fact, one of the first publications to feature her, in August 1994, under the headline "Watch This Girl!"). "The magazines were the result and a manifestation of a '90s version of consciousness raising," wrote Jennifer Baumgardner and Amy Richards in *Manifesta*, "honest talk that spawns more feminism, making connections between women — kind of like a dinner party in print or on the Web."

San Francisco writer Steve Joyner became the guest of honor at that party after ABC announced it was putting *MSCL* on hiatus in December 1994. The 27-year-old fan started what *People* magazine quaintly referred to at the time as "an e-mail drive" to appeal to ABC. "It's the first on-line lobby created to save a television show," the *Baltimore Sun* reported at the time. The campaign reportedly boasted more than 10,000 supporters and raised thousands of dollars to take out ads in *Daily Variety* and the *Hollywood Reporter* urging ABC to keep *MSCL* alive. The show that legitimized teen voices also galvanized teens to use them, turning them into activists. Joyner called the campaign "Operation . . . Life Support" and only a month after it kicked off, ABC president Ted Harbert logged on to AOL to chat with the group. As Joyner told the *Baltimore Sun* at the time, "We've generated more publicity for *My So-Called Life* in a month than ABC has all season." And though ABC executive officer Brian McAndrews told *Entertainment Weekly* that the thousands of protest letters and AOL postings were "not statistically significant," MTV heard Operation . . . Life Support's alarm. On April 10, 1995, the network, aimed at 12- to 34-year-olds, aired *MSCL* Monday through Friday for four weeks (with intros by the various cast members). Two months later, Showtime acquired the Canadian rights, and the show premiered in Canada on September 19, 1995, attracting a whole new set of fans who saw red over its cancellation.

On *MSCL*'s 10th anniversary, *Entertainment Weekly* claimed that the ABC series had "defined the modern family drama." It seemed Holzman had done what she intended to do and given her characters their due as human beings because the show was praised primarily for its authenticity, for its ability to continually introduce tropes and dismantle them, reflecting the true complexity of teen girls and the world. "It's the most painfully honest portrayal of adolescence ever on television," said Greg Berlanti, who created the soft-focus family drama *Everwood* and the teen-centric *Jack & Bobby* (about the Kennedys as adolescents). He confessed that "at least once a week" the writers on his series referenced *MSCL*. In fact, the show seemed to form the backbone of the entire Warner Bros. Television Network (The WB), which launched the year *MSCL* was canceled and introduced a bevy of teen shows — *Dawson's Creek*, *Gilmore Girls*, *Felicity*, *One Tree Hill* — that targeted a similar demo. "I think most people you talk to will talk about *My So-Called Life*," *One Tree Hill* creator Mark Schwahn told *Buddy TV* in 2006. Of his drama about teen brothers in a fictional North Carolina town, he said, "It's usually about something that's a little more human and quiet, but I learned that from *My So-Called Life*." *Dawson's Creek* creator Kevin Williamson admitted he used the show to sell his own drama in the late '90s about a group of highly articulate adolescents in a fictional Massachusetts town. "I pitched it as *Some Kind of Wonderful* meets *Pump Up the Volume* meets *James at 15* meets *My So-Called Life* meets *Little House on the Prairie*," he said. (His *Vampire Diaries* co-creator, Julie Plec, named her production company My So-Called Company.) Even *The O.C.*

creator Josh Schwartz, whose series was considered even talkier than *Dawson's Creek*, confessed to the *New York Times* that he wanted to make his Fox series (which would have fit just as well on the WB) like *MSCL*.

Suddenly, strong women were a small-screen staple, most notably on J.J. Abrams's *Felicity*, which premiered in 1998. Another WB series, it revolves around an eponymous college student, played by Keri Russell, who follows her Jordan Catalano–like crush to university. Though not quite as headstrong as Angela, Felicity is an equally complex heroine searching for her identity; she's even afforded a voice-over. The two shows shared the same directors, giving them the same look, and the same composer, giving them a similar sound. Other series were less obviously indebted to their predecessor but showcased equally powerful heroines. *Daria*, an animated series about a smart cynical teen who basks in non-conformity, arrived in 1997, and show writer Chris Marcil posited that the genre was the reason it survived and *MSCL* didn't. "*My So-Called Life* tackled some similar themes as *Daria* — you know, the girl who's not the most popular and isn't considered the greatest beauty — and it didn't last," he told the *New York Times*. "I suspect it may have had something to do with the fact that it's hard for people to take something that's as real as that. The success of *90210* is that it is fantasy and everybody really is gorgeous and it's very easy to look at. With animation, it at least makes reality more palatable."

Joss Whedon made his feminism more palatable (literally) by vamping up his 1997 cult series *Buffy the Vampire*

*Slayer.* "The description I like best is *My So-Called Life* meets *The X-Files*," he said, adding of the titular blond sun-kissed Sunnydale sophomore, "She is a good role model for not just girls but for everybody, because she has to use her wits and her physical strength to win." Similarly genre-heavy was *Veronica Mars*, created by Rob Thomas in 2004, which follows a teen private eye with a not-so-secret penchant for pop culture (and processed nosh) as she investigates her best friend's murder. The loquacious noir blesses its heroine with not only a face that would definitely make the top 40, but an equally attractive (cerebrally speaking) voice-over. (Thomas was actually considered as a writer for *MSCL* before the show was canceled.) Meanwhile, Judd Apatow, whose slightly less vibrant *Freaks and Geeks* heroine Lindsay Weir is often compared to Angela, has publicly admitted to being a *MSCL* fan numerous times. More recently, his protégé Lena Dunham used *MSCL's* realism as a model for her own smart, unvarnished series about four female friends. "I think *My So-Called Life* and *Felicity* were the shows that really spoke to what I was going through. They influenced me the most," she told *Parade* in 2014, adding, "The characters really made me feel like they understood what it was like to be me, and I understood what it was like to be them. I think I'm always sort of chasing that in my own work."

As with *Felicity*, behind-the-scenes personnel from *MSCL* popped up in various subsequent series, bringing to each of them aspects of Liberty High. Creator/writer Winnie Holzman and her daughter went on to conceive *Huge* for ABC in 2010, which featured Nikki Blonsky as a self-loving teen who does not love fat camp. Playwright Jason Katims, who most notably wrote the *MSCL* episode "Life of Brian," joined the pros as the head writer of *Friday Night Lights* in 2006. The gridiron drama is famous for tackling complex female characters (music again by *MSCL*'s W.G. Snuffy Walden) and, like *MSCL*, is considered one of many that ended too soon. "When I think about *My So-Called Life*," WB regular Greg Berlanti told *Entertainment Weekly*, "I think about that line in *Star Wars*, when Obi-Wan Kenobi tells Darth Vader, 'If you strike me down, I shall become more powerful than you can possibly imagine.' That's exactly what happened here." But, thanks to Angela Chase, she's no longer our only hope.

# <sup>*</sup>Sources

Adalian, Josef. "Vulture Asks Claire Danes Some Burning Questions About *My So-Called Life*," *Vulture*, August 4, 2011.

Baumgardner, Jennifer, and Amy Richards. *Manifesta: Young Women, Feminism, and the Future (10th Anniversary Edition)*. New York: Farrar, Strauss and Giroux, 2010.

Becker, Ron. *Gay TV and Straight America*. New Brunswick: Rutgers University Press, 2006.

Berkshire, Geoff. "*My So-Called Life* Creator Winnie Holzman on Boys Wearing Eyeliner," *Variety*, August 19, 2015.

Bikini Kill. "What Is Riot Grrrl?" *Girl Power*, 1991.

Brockes, Emma. "The Secret Diary of Claire Danes," *The Guardian*, April 2, 2011.

Byers, Michele, and David Lavery. *Dear Angela: Remembering My So-Called Life*. Lanham: Lexington Books, 2007.

Callahan, Maureen. "Watch This Girl!" *Sassy*, August 1994.

Cruz, Wilson. "What Am I? Actor Wilson Cruz: My Identity Is My Sword," *NBC Latino*, May 13, 2013.

Danes, Claire. "Lena Dunham," *Interview*, April 11, 2012.

Danko, Meredith. "22 Things You Might Not Know About *Dawson's Creek*," *Mental Floss*, January 12, 2016.

Dooley, Savannah. "Finding My So-Called Queer Identity in *My So-Called Life*," *TIME*, August 25, 2014.

Dooley, Savannah. "In My So-Called Life," *The Advocate*, July 5, 2005.

Douglas, William. *Television Families: Is Something Wrong in Suburbia?* New York: Routledge, 2003.

Emami, Gazelle. "Elisabeth Moss on Discovering Who She Would Date on *Mad Men*: 'I Fucking Flipped Out,'" *Vulture*, April 5, 2015.

Endrst, James. "Their So-Called Explanations for Death of *Life*," *Hartford Courant*, May 19, 1995.

"Exclusive Interview: Mark Schwahn, Creator/Head Writer of *One Tree Hill*," *BuddyTV*, November 29, 2006.

Findlen, Barbara. *Listen Up: Voices from the Next Feminist Generation (New Expanded Edition)*. Berkeley: Seal Press, 1995.

Friedan, Betty. *The Feminine Mystique (50th Anniversary Edition)*. New York: W. W. Norton & Company, 2013.

Gay, Roxane. *Bad Feminist: Essays*. New York: Harper Perennial, 2014.

Gevinson, Tavi. "Still Figuring It Out," *TEDx Talks*, April 9, 2012.

Giles, Jeff. "The Open Secret — In a Rare Interview, Jaye Davidson Leaves Nothing to the Imagination When Discussing the Oscar-Nominated Film, *The Crying Game*," *The Seattle Times*, March 22, 1993.

Gilligan, Carol. *In a Different Voice*. Cambridge: Harvard University Press, 1993.

Gilligan, Carol. *Making Connections*. Cambridge: Harvard University Press, 1990.

Gliatto, Tom. "Acting Her Age," *People*, October 3, 1994.

Goldstein, Jessica. "*My So-Called Life*'s Wilson Cruz on Rickie Fans, LBGT Awareness, and '90s Fashion," *Vulture*, September 5, 2014.

Gopalan, Nisha. "*My So-Called Life* Revisited," *Entertainment Weekly*, October 25, 2007.

Graham, Jane. "Jared Leto: 'The Gun and Cocaine Moment Was a Turning Point,'" *The Big Issue*, July 31, 2013.

Grow, Kory. "Blister in the Sun Is Not About Masturbation: A Talk with Violent Femmes," *Village Voice*, September 12, 2013.

Gutierrez, Eric. "Cruz Control," *The Advocate*, September 28, 1999.

Hill, Erin. "Lena Dunham on *Girls* and Why Hollywood 'Is Like a Monstrous Sixth Grade,'" *Parade*, January 10, 2014.

hooks, bell. *Teaching to Transgress: Education as the Practice of Freedom*. New York: Routledge, 1994.

"Jared Leto," *People*, May 8, 1995.

Kamen, Paula. "*Transparent*'s Jill Soloway on Inventing the Female Gaze," *Ms.*, November 6, 2014.

Kim, Wook. "Life in the Slow Lane: 10 Memorable TV Small Towns," *TIME*, January 20, 2013.

Kolbert, Elizabeth. "A Female Holden Caulfield for the 1990's," *New York Times*, August 14, 1994.

Kunkel, Dale. Kirstie M. Cope, and Carolyn Colvin. "Sex, Kids and the Family Hour: A Three Part Study of Sexual Content on Television," *The Kaiser Family Foundation*, November 30, 1996.

Kuzynski, Alex. "Beavis and Butt-head's Feminine Side," *New York Times*, May 11, 1998.

Lahr, John. "Varieties of Disturbance," *New Yorker*, September 9, 2013.

Lowry, Dennis T., and Jon A. Shidler. "Prime Time TV Portrayals of Sex, 'Safe Sex' and AIDS: A Longitudinal Analysis," *Journalism & Mass Communication Quarterly*, Autumn 1993.

Martin, Denise. "Geeking Out Over the *My So-Called Life* Finale with Creator Winnie Holzman," *Vulture*, September 5, 2014.

Martin, Denise. "Plaid Shirts and Bib Overalls: The Complete History of Angela's *My So-Called Life* Wardrobe," *Vulture*, September 5, 2014.

Matheson, Frankie. "*My So-Called Life:* Never Before Seen Images & Stories," *Refinery29*, August 28, 2014.

Mendoza, Manuel. "Cruz Gives Character *Life* of Experience as TV First," *Dallas Morning News*, December 22, 1994.

Mendoza, Manuel. "Reality Bites; Latinos Want Fewer TV Stereotypes, More Truth," *Dallas Morning News*, September 18, 1994.

Misener, Jessica. "Brian Krakow From *My So-Called Life* Is Hot Now," *BuzzFeed*, July 21, 2014.

Mulvey, Laura. "Visual Pleasure and Narrative Cinema," *Screen* 16 (3): 6–18, 1975.

Noxon, Marti. "Portrayals of Gays on Mainstream TV and the Future of Gay Cable Channels," *Talk of the Nation*, NPR, January 24, 2002. Radio Transcript.

Pitre, Sarah. "*My So-Called Life*: Cast Reunion," *Forever Young Adult*, June 14, 2013.

Posner, Ari. "No Experience Required," *New York Times*, March 21, 2004.

Reed, J.D. "Cyberchat," *People*, February 13, 1995.

Rich, Katey. "20 Years After *My So-Called Life*, Bess Armstrong Reveals What Creators Planned For Season Two," *Vanity Fair*, August 25, 2014.

Roberts, Soraya. "Television's Safe Sex Problem," *Toronto Star*, April 11, 2013.

Rosenthal, Phil. "*My So-Called Life* in Danger Despite Great Danes," *Los Angeles Daily News*, January 19, 1995.

Seitz, Matt Zoller. "Never Trust a Narrator Who's Under 16," *New York Times*, October 30, 1994.

Sessums, Kevin. "Great Danes," *Vanity Fair*, February 1998.

Shaw, Jessica. "Rabid Fans Show Support for *My So-Called Life*," *Entertainment Weekly*, January 20, 1995.

Van Gelder, Sadie. "Claire Danes," *Seventeen*, September 1995.

Walker, Rebecca. "Becoming the Third Wave," *Ms.*, January 1992.

Ward, L. Monique. "Talking About Sex: Common Themes about Sexuality in the Prime-Time Television Programs Children and Adolescents View Most," *The Journal of Youth and Adolescence*, vol. 24, no. 5, 1995.

Weber, Lindsey. "Devon Gummersall on Being Brian Krakow in a *Mad Men* World," *Vulture*, April 6, 2015.

Weiss, Sasha. "Generation Cry Face," *New Yorker*, November 11, 2012.

Wolf, Naomi. *The Beauty Myth*. Toronto: Vintage Canada, 1997.

Young, Iris Marion. *On Female Body Experience: "Throwing Like a Girl" and Other Essays*. Oxford: Oxford University Press, 2005.

Zuckerman, Esther. "Devon Gummersall on Peggy Olson/ Brian Krakow Fan-Fiction and the *Mad Men* Parts He Didn't Get," *Vanity Fair*, April 6, 2015.

Zurawik, David. "ABC Goes On-Line for *So-Called Life*," *The Baltimore Sun*, January 19, 1995.

## Acknowledgments

If I hadn't first written for *Bitch* about *My So-Called Life*, this book wouldn't have existed. Thank you to Andi Zeisler for accepting the piece and, in fact, for accepting me as an intern two decades ago, which made me want to write about all of this stuff in the first place. She continues to be one of the only people I would ever — without irony — call a mentor.

ECW editors Jen Knoch and Crissy Calhoun for having the patience for all the neuroses involved in writing a first book and for being as inspiring and fashionable as Vic Racine.

Thanks to Winnie Holzman, obviously, for creating a show that formed so many of us and for taking the time to speak with me about it, despite having done so a million times before, and for not vomiting when I asked her, "Are you a feminist?" And a tip of the hat to Shout Factory for sending me the *MSCL* box set and to Michele Byers and David Lavery for editing the one and only *MSCL* essay collection, *Dear Angela*, which was indelible to this book. As well, drummer Mel Lipsey for his analysis of the Violent Femmes.

To the Rayanne Graffs and Rickie Vasquezes who supported me through the various stages of this book: Talia Acker, Leila Ashtari, Mauri Bell, Anne-Marie Bissada, Sarah Butterill, Nicole Liao, Emily Materick, Shaun Pett, Andrea Ryer, Christine Sulek-Popov, and Teri Vlassopoulos.

To my father, Jeremy Roberts, and my grandmother, Zubaida Khatoon, for passing down their love of pop culture. To Heather Young for always asking about it. To my brother, Clifford Roberts, in particular, for letting me know at 15 that Claire Danes wasn't prettier than me, and for, 20 years later, continuing to be one of the biggest supporters of my work and life.

And to my mom, Nasreen Roberts, for everything, and my better half, Christopher Manson, for everything else.

Soraya Roberts still feels like a teenager even though she's, like, old. She worked as an entertainment editor from 2005 to 2011 and is now a full-time writer. She has contributed long-form culture articles to *Hazlitt*, *Harper's*, and the *Los Angeles Review of Books*, among other publications. She also appears in the anthology *Secret Loves of Geek Girls* (Bedside Press, 2015) and is currently working on a memoir about journalism. She lives in Toronto.